Understanding
Addiction as
Self Medication

Understanding Addiction as Self Medication

Finding Hope Behind
the Pain

Edward J. Khantzian, M.D., and
Mark J. Albanese, M.D.

ROWMAN & LITTLEFIELD PUBLISHERS, INC.
Lanham · Boulder · New York · Toronto · Plymouth, UK

ROWMAN & LITTLEFIELD PUBLISHERS, INC.

Published in the United States of America
by Rowman & Littlefield Publishers, Inc.
A wholly owned subsidary of The Rowman & Littlefield Publishing Group, Inc.
4501 Forbes Boulevard, Suite 200, Lanham, Maryland 20706
www.rowmanlittlefield.com

Estover Road
Plymouth PL6 7PY
United Kingdom

British Library Cataloguing in Publication Information Available

Library of Congress Cataloging-in-Publication Data:

Khantzian, Edward J.
  Understanding addiction as self medication : finding hope behind the pain/ Edward
J. Khantzian and Mark J. Albanese.
    p. ; cm.
  Includes bibliographical references and index.
  ISBN-13: 978-0-7425-6137-3 (cloth : alk. paper)
  ISBN-10: 0-7425-6137-2 (cloth : alk. paper)
  eISBN-13: 978-0-7425-6551-7
  eISBN-10: 0-7425-6551-3
  1. Substance abuse. 2. Self medication. 3. Compulsive behavior. I. Albanese, Mark J.,
1961- II. Title.
  [DNLM: 1. Substance-Related Disorders—psychology. 2. Behavior, Addictive—
psychology. 3. Self Medication—psychology. WM 270 K45u 2008]

  RC564.K536 2008
  616.86—dc22   2008015248

Printed in the United States of America

⊗™ The paper used in this publication meets the minimum requirements of
American National Standard for Information Sciences—Permanence of Paper
for Printed Library Materials, ANSI/NISO Z39.48-1992.

For CarolAnn, Nancy Jo, Susan, Jane, and John

E. J. K.

For Jeni, Ariana, Elena, Chiara, Marcus, Ian, and Maya

M. J. A.

Perhaps it took a little time, but it seemed to happen instantly. He could feel his body relaxing, a stiffness going out of his shoulders as he sensed the warm glow seeping through him in all the distant forgotten corners of his being . . .
It was a miracle. There was no other word. A miracle that was affecting him mentally, physically, and, as he would soon learn, spiritually.

Bill W.'s first experience with alcohol as reported to his biographer, Robert Thomsen

Contents

Foreword

$\mathcal{A}$ddiction is one of the most compelling disorders because it is devastating not only to individuals, but to their entire networks of family and friends. While much is heralded about the etiologies of substance use disorders (SUDs), it has become increasingly evident that there are multiple intersecting pathways by which an individual seemingly develops an addiction. Moreover, once somebody is addicted, an entirely separate set of events or stressors may perpetuate the addiction. Not surprisingly, the ability to predict who will recover relatively easily and who will struggle with the perils of an addiction their entire life—perhaps suffering severe morbidity or even death—continues to remain elusive.

One of the most compelling theories to explain the initiation, persistence, and successful remission from SUD is the self-medication hypothesis (SMH) of addictive disorders. As Drs. Khantzian and Albanese clearly describe throughout this book, when addicted individuals resort to addictive drugs, more than anything, they are self-medicating their distress. This approach is helpful both conceptually and practically, in terms of better understanding the addicted person and the role the addiction may play in his or her life. The SMH integrates developmentally inherent vulnerabilities, psychological distress, and life events. Having been exposed to the self-medication notion during my professional development, I often examine the role that substances may be playing in an individual's life—be it to relieve disturbing symptoms or, more covertly, to diminish underlying unbearable feelings.

As a psychiatrist for both children and adults, and as both a clinician and researcher, I am always examining what factors contribute to the development, maintenance, and remission of both SUDs and psychopathology. I am also interested in the critical impact prevention and early intervention will have on those contributing factors, and, ultimately, on the outcomes. When I examine issues around self-medication and SUDs, I am struck by the growing literature to support this connection. In our own work at the Massachusetts General Hospital and Harvard Medical School, we have studied both attention deficit hyperactivity disorder (ADHD) and childhood-onset bipolar disorder, both disorders with problems of inhibition and affective dysregulation, and have shown them to be risk factors for later SUD.

That self-medication may constitute a separate risk or vulnerability that increases the likelihood of an SUD is not surprising, given our better understanding of biological, including genetic, and psychosocial interactions. For example, our group has examined the notion of a disorder like ADHD increasing one's vulnerability to SUD. Not surprisingly, we have found that risk seems to be particularly high, depending on specific interactions with the environment. In the case of ADHD, for instance, we have shown that SUD is increased in young adolescents whose parents are currently using substances or who are at the extremes of social class. Furthermore, among the people with ADHD that we treat, while some report using substances just to get high, the vast majority indicate they are "self-medicating" distress associated with psychiatric symptoms.

We are moving beyond the dichotomous notion of addiction being caused and maintained by either purely biological/genetic or psychosocial roots. There is ample evidence, as described by Drs. Khantzian and Albanese, that these processes are not mutually exclusive, but in fact interactive and developmental in affecting an individual's addiction. Someone who has a family history of addiction is clearly at higher risk for using and ultimately becoming addicted to a compound. It may be that the presence of, for example, self-care deficits or prominent psychological trauma may further predispose those individuals to developing addictive behaviors that will initially relieve, but ultimately exacerbate their psychosocial dysfunction. Moreover, the substances affect brain biology that promotes addiction, further exacerbating self-blame, shame, depression, anxiety, and psychosocial chaos. Invariably, to halt this process, both biological and psychological interventions are necessary. Thus addicted individuals need help to reduce the craving or use, and to identify and begin treating underlying conditions that set them up for relapse. As described throughout the book, the challenge of optimal treatment for addiction continues to reside in a truly multimodal model. Such a model focuses not only on the important biology of the addiction, but also on the individual's real-life needs and requirements, psychiatric symptoms, and stressors in the environment.

While there are different ways to understand addiction, as practitioners we strive for common ground and improved outcomes for our patients who suffer from addictive disorders. Our goal is that they emerge not only free of the substance but in better emotional health, which promotes remission and overall wellness. In this regard, Drs. Khantzian and Albanese keenly provide insight to understanding the intricacies of the psyche and interactions of vulnerability that are active in the addictive process. I am sure that all readers, clinicians and non-clinicians alike, will find this book helpful.

Timothy E. Wilens, M.D.
Massachusetts General Hospital,
Harvard Medical School,
and Bay Cove Human Services
Boston, Mass.

Acknowledgments

We would like to thank all of our colleagues—especially at Massachusetts Mental Health Center, Cambridge Health Alliance, Danvers State Hospital, Tewksbury Hospital, and Harvard Medical School—whose invaluable support over the years has fostered a climate making our work, despite the challenges, both possible and doable. We would also like to acknowledge those colleagues and friends, Martin Weegman, Mark Green, Corinne Gerwe, Bill O'Heaney, Josh Marcus, and Mary Nada, who were generous with their time in reading our manuscript and offering invaluable feedback. We are grateful for the support and help of our editor, Sarah Stanton, without whom we would not have completed this project. We are especially appreciative of the diligence and responsiveness with which she took on the completion of this project. We would also like to acknowledge Ashleah Younker and our production editor, Melissa McNitt, for their invaluable assistance in preparing and finalizing the manuscript for production. Three colleagues deserve special credit for what they have taught us and the support and wisdom they have so generously extended to us over the years we have been doing this work: Jan Kauffman, Howard Shaffer, and Gregg Baker. In addition we are pleased and proud that a former student, and now respected colleague, Jesse Suh, has contributed so generously to this book by writing a chapter on the empirical evidence for the self-medication hypothesis. In addition he was generous with his time in reviewing several versions of the chapters in this book. Finally, and most importantly, we want to express our sincerest gratitude to our patients, whose patience with us has been crucial to our growth as clinicians. They have been our best teachers.

Introduction

$\mathcal{A}$ddiction is the biggest single public and mental health problem in modern society. Addiction is consuming in the depth to which it affects individuals, and extensive in the breadth to which it affects persons from all walks of society. This book is intended to reach concerned citizens who are curious as to how and why this is so. These concerned people, their families, or their friends might also have succumbed to addiction and need and want to know how and why it consumed them. It is intended for students and scholars of addictions in that the concept of self-medication is a good idea that needs further study and elaboration. It is also intended for clinicians and counselors who need a humanistic and empathic model to help them engage and understand the patients they treat.

Those who experience addiction, witness it, or treat it cannot avoid the vexing question, "How can I/they continue such a devastatingly destructive behavior?" This applies to the most prevalent addiction, nicotine dependence, as well as its close runner-up, alcohol dependence. It also applies to cocaine, speed, opiates, and the range of party drugs—more recent addictive candidates—which threaten the well-being of young and old. These days activities such as gambling, dieting, fitness, and compulsive sexual behaviors are also conceptualized as addictive in nature. This is so because behavioral addictions share with other addictions the distinctive quality of persistence and recurrence despite deleterious, damaging consequences.

Einstein said our theories help us to identify the facts. Addictive behaviors beg for an informed explanation to guide patients, families, students, and clinicians to help bear with and understand the maddening, puzzling, and often incomprehensible nature of the addictions. In fact there are few if any commonly acceptable theories for addictive behavior which provide a meaningful understanding. One such theory or explanation is the self-medication hypothesis (SMH). A not uncommon description from those familiar with the SMH is that it is "one of the most intuitively appealing theories about drug abuse."[1]

The two authors of this book are the principal developers and proponents of the theory and are widely cited as the authors of the SMH. The SMH is based primarily on extensive clinical experience in working with patients who have suffered with addictive disorders. There is also increasing scientific evidence to support the SMH. There is only one other designated theory, primarily adopted by neuroscientists: the opponent-process theory (OPT)[2] of addictive behavior. The SMH does not compete with OPT, but more likely complements it. The self-medication hypothesis gives a humanistic and understandable explanation as to why addictions are so compelling. It emphasizes that psychological pain is at the heart of addictive behavior and that vulnerable individuals resort to their addiction because they discover that the addictive substance or behavior gives short-term and otherwise unobtainable relief, comfort, or change from their distress. The SMH further suggests that a person's choice of substance or behavior is because the substance or behavior has a specific action or quality which relieves particular feeling states that tend to predominate in that individual.

Although the SMH was updated within the last decade,[3] the authors have not until now translated the helpful perspective offered by the SMH into a common, readable, and readily understandable statement from which members of our society who are affected by addiction can benefit. This book is intended to fill that void.

Why the Self-Medication Hypothesis?

Something in their lives introduced them to substances, and those substances made them feel better than anything else in their life had made them feel, whether their lives were good, which in some cases they were, or very difficult. They felt whole for the first time. They sought that feeling over and over, and disregarded or were unable to notice the pain that they were causing themselves, let alone others. At some point, life got unacceptably bad, and there were too many losses. Their initial efforts to stop were halfhearted until, at some point they recognized they needed major help. Finally, they admitted they were helpless and turned themselves and their will over to a program outside themselves.

Mary Nada, MSW[1]

*A*ddictive behavior is an extremely prevalent, bewildering, and devastating condition. For example, one recent study of the United States population estimated that about 15 percent of adults suffer from an alcohol or drug problem during the course of their lives.[2] Despite the terrible consequences of addiction that affect every aspect of their lives, individuals persist in their addictive behaviors; even after long periods of abstinence many tragically revert back to their addictions. Are there theories or explanations of why addictions are so unrelenting, consuming, and recurrent? Does the problem reside in the brain, the mind, or the person? Are there lessons to be learned from the past century in which we have witnessed heroin, cocaine, Oxycontin, and crystal meth cutting a wide destructive swath across all strata of society? Have hopeful solutions and treatments emerged which might offer clues as to the nature of addictive vulnerability?

These questions about the condition and consequences of addictive behavior beg for answers. We are writing this book because we believe that the experience of addictive illness and recovery from it has much to teach others who experience, witness, and treat it.

We have a particular view for understanding addictive illness. It derives from our approach as two clinician-investigators whose experience totals more than six decades of work and research aimed at fathoming the nature of addictive vulnerability. We have shared a keen interest in understanding, explaining, and treating what it is that makes an addictive drug or behavior so compelling and self-perpetuating. Our approach has been grounded in a seemingly simple question we have posed for ourselves and our patients over the decades we have studied and treated people with addictive disorders, namely, "What does the drug do for you?"* It turns out this "simple" question is not so simple after all. It taps into important aspects of our inner psychological life involving emotions, self-love, and painful relationships which individuals discover can be relieved or changed by addictive substances or behaviors. Posed in this way, the question also provides an empathic means for the clinician and patient to connect in a nonjudgmental way, and to begin to understand why a drug or addictive behavior is so compelling.

Based primarily on clinical work and investigative studies by us and others dating back to the 1970s, this book focuses on the self-medication hypothesis (SMH) of addictive disorders. The SMH has two important aspects to it. First, addictive drugs become addicting because they have the powerful effect of alleviating, removing, or changing human psychological suffering. A second important aspect is that there is a considerable degree of specificity in a person's choice of drugs. Addictive drugs are not universally appealing. Although a person might experiment and use a number of addictive substances, individuals navigate toward a certain drug because of what it does for them.

In fact, individuals do not choose to become dependent on a particular drug. Rather what happens is that an addiction-prone individual, experimenting with various drugs, discovers that he or she is drawn to one of the classes of drugs (e.g., stimulants, depressants, opiate analgesics) because they make the individual feel better than anything else. Drugs interact with troublesome or painful feeling states and personality factors to

---

*The question can be posed as well with behavioral addictions such as compulsively gambling, overeating, exercising to excess, etc. In chapter 11 we will explore some of these conditions in more detail.

make their effects pleasant or unpleasant. In our experience, for example, lethargic individuals who might or might not be depressed welcome the energizing and activating effects of a stimulant drug such as cocaine or "speed" (an amphetamine). Stimulants also have special appeal for hyper-energized and hyperactive individuals. The hyper-energized (manic-like) enjoy or appreciate the boost of stimulants whereas the hyperactive person benefits from the paradoxical calming effects of stimulants. A person who is uptight and uncomfortable about expressing emotion might find repeated low to moderate doses of alcohol appealing because he or she briefly can tolerate such feelings. Higher doses of alcohol may be required to quiet down those who are more extremely tense, anxious, or agitated. And for those who become agitated, angry, and rageful, opiates provide a magical calming and comforting influence. Conversely, some drug effects may be experienced as unwelcome or averse; a controlled person, for example, might experience the loosening effects of alcohol as very uncomfortable and threatening; another person, more anxious and fearful, might react with terror or panic in response to the stimulating properties of cocaine.

Much of the SMH was derived from a psychodynamic perspective, a distilled version of psychoanalytic theory and practice, and further guided by both modern psychiatric diagnostic and treatment considerations and a humanistic approach to the patient. Nevertheless, at its root the SMH of addictive disorders is a psychological theory which provides a useful pathway for understanding the addictions. We believe that it complements, not competes with, biological understandings of addictive processes. Clearly, as evidenced by the fact that most addictions cause physical dependence and tolerance, biological processes are present. Physical dependence refers to the experience of abrupt withdrawal from addictive drugs that causes individuals to experience a range of distressful and potentially life-threatening adverse symptoms and reactions. Physical tolerance refers to the fact that over time more and more of a substance is required to achieve a desired effect. Many experts argue that physical dependence and tolerance give addictions their enormous power. Put more simply, a person drinks or takes drugs a lot because they drink or take drugs a lot; that is, a person might think they want a drink but in fact they need a drink because they need to treat their withdrawal. In our opinion the mechanisms of withdrawal and tolerance are insufficient alone to explain the powerful, compelling, and consuming course of addictive illness. To mention just a few examples, biological mechanisms on their own cannot explain relapse after a person has established abstinence for years, nor account for the fact that many individuals use large and excessive amounts of substances only periodically under certain conditions which are not biologically determined.

Biologically oriented investigators refer to "reward" mechanisms to explain how addictive substances and behaviors are reinforcing and lead to continuation of addictive behaviors. Psychodynamic investigators have emphasized psychological processes that make addictive behavior and relapse so common. It is our opinion that these two perspectives are complementary. In this book we will try to consider, where relevant, how this is the case. Obviously there are other valid psychological perspectives on addictive disorder, such as cognitive-behavioral or dialectic behavior theory. For the most part we will focus on a psychodynamic/psychiatric one because the SMH derives from that perspective.

Throughout this book we will draw on many case examples to demonstrate the nature of some of the main psychological vulnerabilities that in our experience appear to be associated with substance use disorders (SUDs). The cases are composites, and disguised in order to protect the identities of the patients with whom we have worked. Because of our emphasis on psychological vulnerabilities, in many of the cases we make note of childhood histories of trauma, neglect, and abuse. As we will emphasize throughout this book, the determinants for the development of SUDs involve an interaction of biological, psychological, and environmental factors. For some the preponderance of vulnerability is biological; for others the determinants are primarily external. In many, but not all, of the clinical cases, we describe the role of parental neglect or abuse and traumatizing environments in the development of an addictive disorder. Needless to say there are many cases, in our own experience and that of others, where there does not seem to be neglect or abuse associated with the development of an addiction. Parental neglect or abuse is not necessary for the development of an SUD, but their presence makes SUDs more likely. Furthermore, experience has shown that parents can and do impact their children in a positive way, protecting them from the development of SUDs.

Around the time we completed this book, the *Washington Post* published a thoughtful and provocative article by a journalist who discussed openly what had driven her addiction.[3] She indicated that she started to use drugs to address her social isolation, and then she settled on heroin to "self-medicate" her distress. The heroin "always soothed and smoothed" her distress, which was ultimately treated with antidepressant medication. She reviewed the most salient and current understandings of addiction, expressing the view that none of them completely explained her experience. She commented on the strengths and shortcomings of the perspectives she considered. These perspectives included physical dependence aspects of addiction, learning theory, drug-induced changes in the brain, and a disease concept of addiction that requires surrender to a higher power. For example, the past three to four decades have produced important and exciting neuroscientific findings on many aspects of brain functions and processes that explain important aspects of addictions and how addictive drugs and behaviors interact in the brain. At its roots this approach is a biological theory of addiction.

At the end of her article the author concluded that what matters the most is the view that produces compassion and effective treatment. We agree with her. We believe the perspective offered by the SMH bridges and corrects for many of the gaps and flaws pointed out in the *Washington Post* article. Thus, while biological psychiatry has produced extraordinary discoveries regarding what drugs do *in the brain*, the SMH attempts to understand what drugs do *in the person and for the person*. No explanation of what makes addictive behavior so devastatingly compelling is complete without accounting for what drugs do for a person, a dimension of addictive behavior which has received far too little attention. The SMH also provides the needed compassion and a basis to consider what is necessary to make treatment successful. This book intends to fill this gap for those who suffer with addictive disorder and look for a humanistic psychological understanding of their condition. It is also intended for those—such as friends, family members, clinicians, and scholars—who are similarly puzzled and concerned as they witness the consuming effects of addictive illness.

· 2 ·

Addiction: Disease or Disorder

$\mathcal{S}$cientists and clinicians are guided by theories to help them better understand the nature of problems, and therefore solve them. As we noted in the introduction, Einstein said our theories help us to identify the facts, a point of view which runs counter to the more common belief that facts are the foundation for theories. In the case of a condition such as addiction, a model or theory for understanding it is especially important because the way the condition affects those who suffer with it and those who witness it is subject to horrible misunderstanding and moralistic judgments. Addicted individuals also need a basis to understand how and why they succumbed to and recovered from their disorder, a condition that is derailing and bewildering. We trust this book will provide a basis to appreciate and deal with the intolerance and confusion that addictive illness evokes in those who experience it directly and family and friends who endure it indirectly.

Although addictive disorders have complicated medical and psychiatric aspects, a natural experiment which began in the mid 1930s without considering such complexities began to offer hope and a more sympathetic perspective for understanding alcoholism. An unsuccessful stock broker and a surgeon, both alcoholics, joined together to talk with each other about their inability to not drink and the tragic consequences that resulted. They quickly realized that it would help them and others if they could recruit others to join them in the discussions about how they were powerless over their addictions and needed each other to refrain completely from alcohol. With these humble beginnings Alcoholics Anonymous (AA) was born. Bill W. and Dr. Bob, the founders of AA, provided a way to understand and help hundreds of thousands of individuals who suffered from this condition. They called it a disease and likened the condition to any other medical problem in which a toxic influence such as a poison, allergy, or germ can cause damage to our bodies and minds in a predictable way. Of note, the AA twelve-step approach also has a significant spiritual dimension. This approach, also, is quite beneficial to those who suffer with addictive disorders.

The publication of the *Disease Concept of Alcoholism* by Edward Jelineck in 1962 offered a substantive theory of alcoholism and underscored the idea that it was a legitimate medical condition. The development of AA and the disease concept has had enormous beneficial effects on how addictions are perceived and dealt with in our society. Unfortunately, as often happens with successful ideas, this concept has overshadowed alternative ideas and theories about addiction. The AA approach, which has helped many people with their addictions, is not an approach to which all individuals respond favorably. In fact, studies have demonstrated similar efficacy for other treatment modalities. Given human differences and the heterogeneity of addictive disorders, alternative ways of understanding or theorizing about addictions are necessary. For many people, just avoiding substances of any kind is not sufficient to maintain sobriety. For example, individuals who suffer from psychiatric conditions in addition to an addiction do better when they are treated for both conditions. Typically the treatment involves the prescription of medication for the addiction and psychiatric conditions, as well as various forms of psychotherapy to address the range of issues which have both predisposed them and contributed to the perpetuation of their addictions.

Another important development since the last half of the twentieth century has been the remarkable technical and scientific progress in tracking the anatomy and biology of the brain, including how prescribed and nonprescribed drugs react in the brain. As we emphasized in the first chapter, these discoveries have had a major influence on understanding how addictive drugs affect the brain, but do not adequately explain how they influence a person's emotions, ways of thinking about that experience, and behaviors which perpetuate addictions. The complex interaction of the person, the underlying dysregulation that he or she experiences, and the way an addictive substance serves to address and perpetuate the dysregulation cannot be accounted for by biological models alone.

As we have stated, we present a psychological understanding of addictions which complements the disease and biological understandings, and can offer additional beneficial pathways to conceptualize and treat addictive conditions. Our point of view is also influenced by the fact that we are psychiatrists who have been trained to appreciate how biological, social, psychological, and spiritual factors interact to produce psychiatric disorders. In this respect, based on our clinical experience and that of other clinicians and scientists, we believe that addictions, which have their own unique characteristics, are similar to other psychiatric disorders, such as depression. In addition, over the past several decades psychiatrists have come to appreciate that there is a constant and unusually high association between other psychiatric disorders and addictive disorders. We will discuss this at length in chapter 6. For now, suffice it to say that with all categories of psychiatric disorders, what is often insufficiently appreciated is the enormous amount of psychological pain and suffering associated with them. Nowhere is the pain more evident than in individuals who have suffered major psychological trauma. Van der Kolk has movingly captured this when he says it is a condition in which time fails to heal all wounds.[1] Individuals who have experienced such trauma are much more likely to succumb to addictive disorders. Those who suffer this condition, whether it is the result of childhood sexual or physical abuse, rape, or combat, have lifelong difficulties in containing or regulating their emotions.[2] Emotions are experienced in the extreme; they are either overwhelming and unbearable or numbing and confusing. It should not be surprising that an opiate would calm the agitation associated with this condition, as would an obliterating dose of alcohol, or that cocaine or crystal methamphetamine would alter or relieve the numbing, empty feeling states. We will revisit trauma at greater length in chapter 8.

In addition to these psychiatric conditions, as humans we also suffer a range of painful emotions not associated with a psychiatric disorder that could make the effect of an addictive drug especially appealing. For example, one study has reported on a group of people who had neither an addiction nor a psychiatric disorder. The investigators found that nervousness during the day was associated with an increase in alcohol consumption in the evening. And the alcohol consumption, in turn, was associated with lowered levels of nervousness.[3] For those with a genetic predisposition to addiction, this kind of use could evolve into addiction. We will emphasize repeatedly in this book the idea that human distress and psychological suffering, whether resulting from a psychiatric disorder or not, are at the root of most addictive behavior. While not denying "reward," pleasure, or self-destructive motives for substance use, we will underscore how addictive substances and behaviors can relieve, sooth, calm, or change distress, thus giving them enormous power to dominate and take over a person's life.

The case of Donald is a good example of how both emotional distress and psychiatric conditions can make dependence on addictive drugs so appealing and powerful. He was a thirty-five-year-old man who had been admitted to the hospital for depression and suicidal behavior exacerbated by divorce and job loss. For a man who had suffered much through his life he was surprisingly calm and unexpressive of emotion. He told the doctor who evaluated him that he had been physically and sexually abused from childhood through his teen years—first it was sexual abuse by his biological father when he was a young child, then regular beatings with a belt buckle by his stepfather. Without much prompting by the doctor, he described how addictive drugs had become a regular part of his life from an early age and how these drugs helped him to cope with and tolerate the pain and discomfort his traumatic experiences were causing him. He mentioned how he got drunk as a young child when he drank one of his parent's unfinished drinks. His parents laughed when they realized what had happened. He recalled how good the alcohol made him feel. By age fourteen he was regularly experimenting with and using alcohol, marijuana, hallucinogens, and speed. As a late teen he regularly drank large amounts of alcohol and had used heroin off and on for a number of years. He said he felt "exhilarated" when he first tried freebase cocaine and that heroin had a calming and soothing effect on his irritability and rage (feelings which are not uncommon with individuals who experienced trauma). When the evaluating doctor asked him to describe further what else the heroin did for him, he said that all his inner constant discomfort disappeared. This same doctor observed firsthand how much calmer and less irritable Donald became after the prescription opioid analgesic Oxycodone was prescribed for severe hip pain. Donald explained that he had used heavy doses of alcohol—a cheap, but less effective alternative to heroin— over his adult life to dampen inner states of nervousness, general emotional discomfort, and violent feelings. Sometimes this discomfort took physical forms, such as abdominal complaints and worsening of his very real hip pain.

Henry Krystal, one of the early authorities on post-traumatic stress disorders, referred to the "endless suffering" associated with traumatic experiences.[4] As extreme as this case sounds, it is not uncommon and typifies the lifelong dilemmas such patients experience. Donald was diagnosed with a personality disorder, major depression, post-traumatic stress disorder, and somatic disorder. What typically gets lost in such cases, often as a consequence of off-putting personality characteristics, is what Dr. Krystal refers to as the persistent and extreme suffering that individuals like

Donald endure. Donald made it clear that psychological and physical pain and suffering were constants in his life, taking both subtle and overt forms. He also displayed the flip-flop in emotions, alternating between indifference and rageful outbursts, commonly seen with traumatic disorders. As with other trauma patients, his sleep hours were invaded by distressing flashbacks and repetitious nightmares about his traumatic experiences. It is not uncommon to hear how substance use and abuse interacts with the patients' inner emotional turmoil and provides temporary relief from their distress. This case also typifies the tragic repetitions that occur into adulthood, disrupting social and work life. The human tragedy of cases like Donald's gets lost in debates about diagnoses, their believability, and the stigmatization of "drug abuse," when in fact what is begged for here is a measure of empathy for patients' suffering and their need to resort to drug solutions and other misbehaviors that are too often confusing, off-putting, and self-defeating. In chapters 3, 7, and 8 we will further examine the role of emotional distress in the evolution of addictions.

We have placed a deliberate emphasis in this chapter on viewing and understanding addiction as a disorder with underlying psychological distress, often associated with psychiatric disorders. Donald's case is a powerful example of the all-too-frequent tragedies which we clinicians repeatedly encounter in our work. We have not expanded on the biological effects of addictive drugs on the brain and the rest of the body. As we indicated in chapter 1, the disease nature of addictions, and the biological mechanisms underlying the disease, are clear, but cannot alone explain why addictions are so compelling. Rather, what we feel needs more elaboration, and what we focus on in this book, is how our nature as human beings, with our penchant to suffer a range of painful emotional states, causes us to be vulnerable to the captivating and compelling effects of addictive drugs and behaviors, which have the ability to change, relieve, or eliminate short-term psychological distress and suffering.

The SMH and Addiction as a Problem in Self-Regulation

As we have been saying, suffering is at the heart of addictions. People who become addicted suffer because they have difficulty regulating their (1) emotions; (2) sense of self-worth; (3) relationships; and (4) behaviors, especially self-care. While much has been written about how the widespread availability of addictive drugs, their pleasure-producing effects, and the human proclivity for self-destruction make addiction likely, our clinical experience convincingly demonstrates that the short-term ability of addictive substances to relieve, change, or make more tolerable the distress associated with the problems of dysregulated emotions, self-worth, relationships, and behaviors powerfully reinforces dependence on the substance. People who know and are comfortable about their feelings, like themselves, get along easily with others, and are careful about their behaviors are not apt to become addicted, notwithstanding an overwhelming genetic predisposition.

TONY THE BARBER—NOT KNOWING

Tony has been in recovery from alcohol and cocaine dependence for fifteen years. He is proud of how far he has come with the help of AA and counseling. He's a talkative and jovial man, but he wasn't always that way. He says that during the days he was addicted, he was an angry, wild man who was reckless and unpredictable about where he went, what he did, and the people with whom he associated. In looking back on that time he says he was lost when it came to knowing his feelings and how important a part of life they were. He says that early in recovery his counselor would ask him what he felt about important events in his life, such as his mother's death, and repeatedly he would say, "I don't know, I don't know, I don't know!" He says it was always hard for him to be in touch with his feelings, and when upsetting events would happen he was likely to do something impulsive, get angry, or run away. Working with his counselor over a long period of time he evolved from saying, "Maybe I feel" to "I think I feel" to "I feel." When he talks about this he stammers and stumbles and is embarrassed to realize how out of touch and confused he was about his emotional life. He says that as he got better, his challenge was to stick with feeling his feelings, especially those that were painful and uncomfortable. He says his counseling and AA meetings in particular have helped him to recognize his emotions better and to realize that he is not unique in being confused and avoidant when it comes to dealing with and accepting distress.

Although one might be surprised that such basic aspects of life as being aware of and in touch with feelings could be as confusing and intolerable as they were for Tony, those who treat addicted people commonly encounter these issues. The appeal of addictive drugs, depending on the drug and a person's reaction to it, is that they can blot out feelings, intensify them, or simply change them. When people are not as emotionally dysregulated as Tony, they can recognize and distinguish among emotions like anxiety and depression, and can accept that such emotions are an unavoidable part of life. In Tony's case, he not only could not come up with words for what he was feeling, but often tended to experience and express his distress through impulsive actions and in vague bodily symptoms and discomfort, again not an unusual response for individuals who suffer with addictive problems. While the way individuals use addictive drugs to cope with emotions is initially helpful and the benefits short-term, the effect is powerful enticement and what often sets the hook for vulnerable individuals. The problem is that using more and more drugs to achieve emotional regulation deepens the dependency, leading to atrophy of any self-regulatory skills, and physical dependence in which withdrawal—that is, coming off the drug—further reinforces the addiction. In the end, the difficulties dealing with feelings are made worse, compounded by the pain of withdrawal. In this way, addictions take on a life of their own, drug use begetting more drug use in an endless spiral.

A generation of psychoanalysts and psychodynamic psychiatrists in the mid to late twentieth century have discovered that feelings are neither a given nor uniformly the same for all individuals. Where Freud in the late nineteenth and early twentieth centuries stressed the role of drives, the unconscious, and the repression of feelings and thoughts, contemporary researchers have discovered that feelings, like other aspects of psychological development, progress in more or less predictable ways. When there are major damaging or neglectful experiences either growing up or later in life, the capacity to experience and know one's emotions can be damaged. Thus, someone like Tony is not so much blocking out or denying feelings, which early Freudian theory would suggest, but instead displaying a deficit in psychological development. In other words there is a problem or disorder in knowing, naming, and feeling feelings. Peter Sifneos, an American psychoanalyst of Greek lineage, drawing on his ethnic heritage, with John Nemish, coined the term "alexithymia"[1] to capture this deficit; the prefix "a" referring to the absence of, "lex" referring to words, and "thymia" referring to feelings. Literally translated it means "no words for feelings." In our own work we have referred to this distressful, confusing, and vague experience of feelings as "dysphoria." The SMH emphasizes that addictive drugs and behaviors relieve this dysphoria associated with painful or confusing feelings, with which patients like Tony suffer, thus reinforcing the appeal of those substances and behaviors.

In contrast to Tony's constricted expression of emotion, others are overwhelmed with emotions, and resort to action, activity, and drugs to relieve their intensity and make them more tolerable. We will elaborate more on this aspect of how individuals self-medicate the distress of overwhelming or unbearable emotions in the next chapter.

UNLOVABLE CAROL

Carol is an accomplished pediatrician who had to overcome many obstacles to become a physician. When Carol first came for treatment she was colorfully dressed in black leather pants and a bright red jacket. She smiled frequently and was animated in her manner of speaking. Despite her attractive appearance and likeable manner, as her treatment progressed she revealed a deep insecurity and lack of confidence. She had become dependent on narcotic pain medications prescribed for her sister, for whom she cared while she suffered with terminal cancer. Her sister suggested that Carol try one of her pain pills after a root canal procedure. Carol had the dramatic discovery that the medication not only relieved her physical pain, but it gave her a fantastic emotional lift and sense of well-being.

Carol and her sister both experienced a very troubled upbringing with an alcoholic father who overwhelmed the entire household. Carol had to provide some of the parenting for both herself and her sister. Both of them became over-achievers, Carol as a physician and her sister as a business executive.

One of the main effects on her of those early years was a reservoir of anger and resentment which she said could easily erupt with the slightest provocation. She indicated, "Anger is very tough for me . . . it feels unsafe and at all costs I have to squelch it." In spite of her upbeat and appealing image, she described how insecure she felt and how she always had to project an image of perfection and lovability. Carol explained, "I mustn't let anyone know about that [angry] part of me; they might not approve . . . they might not love me. I must be lovable—absolutely lovable. I have to be absolutely lovable!" The narcotic pain relievers calmed her and would cause her concerns about her lovability to recede.

Our sense of ourselves and how we want others to appreciate us is important enough, but someone like Carol is unsure about her basic lovability. This is a setup for chronic low self-esteem which can affect many aspects of life. Carol's words give ample indication of how such concerns can overtake a person. People such as Carol have experienced how addictive drugs like opioid analgesics calm the rage and anger that shake her confidence in herself. On another day or for another person, a stimulating drug could bolster self-esteem by energizing or helping to initiate contact with someone in order to feel better. For a person struggling with self-confidence problems who is tightly wrapped and defensive about his needs for affection and approval, a low to moderate dose of alcohol could soften him up to accept or invite affection when ordinarily unable to do so.

The psychology of self-love or self-regard is important to understanding the vulnerability to addiction. Much psychological distress derives from not liking ourselves enough, as Carol's case testifies. The self-psychologist Heinz Kohut and his followers[2] were pioneers in the last part of the twentieth century in helping to articulate how problems with self-love can be detrimental to healthy mental life and contribute to a range of troubling behaviors, including addiction. Some try to compensate for their poor self-regard by making too much of themselves, and we unflatteringly characterize such individuals as "narcissists." In contrast, certain individuals make too much of others and derive their sense of well-being from them. In the case of the addiction-prone who struggle with such issues of self-regard, addictive substances become the object of their love and provide a means to feel better about themselves.

RESERVED JEFF

Jeff is an appealing forty-seven-year-old production manager who had a long history of alcohol and cocaine dependence. He recalls that in high school he was shy and reserved, until he discovered the lubricating effects of alcohol. Jeff said, "Alcohol allowed me to get outside myself . . . to put aside my reserved character." Without it he said he was "retiring and quiet . . . drinking I could express myself better and I was better company."

During his twenties he cut back significantly, drinking only occasionally and moderately. He describes himself reverting to a drab, grey existence during this period. In his thirties he discovered cocaine. Jeff said, "It allowed me to be a lot of things I had been in the past . . . my energy returned, I had a sense of humor and felt like a worthy companion again." He said previously he had been isolated, cut off, and avoiding social situations. Although the cocaine worked for awhile, as his use escalated he started to drink heavily again, all leading up to admitting himself for detoxification and rehabilitation. After his rehab stay, although he did not drink or use drugs, he found himself reverting to his old uncommunicative and isolative habits, not speaking with his wife and cutting himself off socially, not reaching out to the few friends he had. He started taking the antidepressant Prozac around five years out of rehab. Subsequently, he has been able to communicate better—"the words now come out unfiltered . . . I even look forward to going home from work to see my wife."

Relationships can be some of the most satisfying and bedeviling aspects of our existence as human beings. As much as we are social creatures, we can also be avoidant of relationships, even when we most need them. Some of us are better than others at relationships. For those less able to connect to others, life can be dreary, lonely, and depressing, as Jeff's life was for long stretches of time. Unfortunately, individuals such as Jeff are susceptible to the discovery that alcohol can temporarily fix their relationship difficulties. One view of addiction is that it is an "attachment disorder."[3] Establishing and maintaining meaningful relationships, an essential aspect of life, provides a sense of comfort, safety, and security. As with so many personality components, the capacity to connect to others reflects back to inborn temperament and early parental relationships. Starting with the earliest phases of development, a lifelong challenge for human beings is to work out relationships in a satisfactory and satisfying way. Unfortunately for some, the capacity to relate to others gets derailed early in life, and addictions can be substituted for the comfort and well-being that relationships can provide.

CARELESS CARL

Carl was a skilled carpenter. The care he took in his craft contrasted sharply with how he took care of himself. His clients were consistently pleased with the care and attention he devoted to his work, whether it was in fashioning a special cabinet or completing the finish-work in a redesigned room. Yet when it came to billing for his projects he often lost his receipts or the accounting for the hours he and his workmen put into a job. He also often misplaced the keys to his pickup truck when starting out in the morning, leading to endless turmoil in his family as they helped him get organized and out the door for his day's work. Carl also caused havoc in his personal finances—not balancing his checking account and overdrawing, missing insurance payments, and losing important financial documents. He also was subject to accidental falls and scrapes because he often moved and jumped ahead of himself before checking his surroundings.

Carl was not dependent on alcohol, but he overused and abused it, often causing him embarrassment when he was with family or friends. Despite knowing his tendencies, he repeatedly behaved in silly or inappropriate ways, especially when he drank. Though often bemoaning his fate as a "loser" after such occurrences, he seemed incapable of anticipating trouble associated with situations, people, and things that would cause him embarrassment and remorse when he drank too much or was excessive in his behaviors. Some of his excesses were a function of his need to be super-friendly and likeable. But the main difficulty seemed to be obliviousness to cues and warnings that a given situation or relationship could lead to problematic behavior.

Anxiety and worry are inescapable in life. When excessive, they can be paralyzing; when absent, they can leave individuals in harm's way, as seems to be the case with Carl. In several decades of trying to understand the bases of addictive vulnerability, we have been impressed repeatedly with how vital functions which insure our existence and safety, such as appropriate concern and worry, are often deficient or absent in people like Carl. Some theorists, including early psychoanalysts, believe survival reactions are instinctive and that accidents reflect unconscious drives. In our experience, such survival mechanisms are neither instinctive nor necessarily reflect unconscious motives, but rather develop out of the early environment in which the child gradually learns from her parents to be vigilant and aware of harm and danger, and to take action to address or avoid situations that might be harmful or dangerous. In damaging or neglectful growing up environments such capacities are more often compromised. We have designated theses functions as the "capacity for self-care."[4] Not insignificantly, neuroscientists using neuroimaging techniques have documented how methamphetamine abusers who relapsed showed less activation in regions of the brain (prefrontal and temporal cortex and the insula) involving choice and action, than did abusers who did not relapse. This is one more example of how findings from neuroscience can complement and support what we learn from clinical experience.[5] People like Carl are vulnerable to excessive and aberrant behaviors, including addictive behaviors with all their unwanted results, because their underdeveloped capacity for self-care causes them to not be anxious or worried enough about hazards in potential and actual dangerous situations. While we cannot deny unconscious self-destructive motives and instincts, we have found, from our developmental perspective, that self-harm is frequently the result of an underdeveloped or absent capacity for self-care.

Individuals who succumb to addictions are often referred to as having an "addictive personality." Aside from being an unflattering and unempathic portrayal, such a description detracts from the preeminently human vulnerabilities involved in addictive problems. We do not subscribe to the notion of an addictive personality. Rather it is our experience and conviction that addictions involve conditions in which problems with regulating emotions, self-love, relationships, and self-care interact in varying degrees with each other, genetic vulnerability, and the environment, depending on the individual, to make addiction more likely. For Tony the barber, it was the bewildering nature of emotions which, in combination with reckless and careless behavior, led to his involvement with and addiction to cocaine. In the case of Carol, her need to be loved and accepted at all times made narcotic painkillers enticing. In Jeff's case, the difficulty in connecting to others, and related problems with isolation and depression, made alcohol and cocaine all too attractive a means to relate to others when it was otherwise impossible. And finally, is it surprising that someone like Carl, so out of touch with hazards and dangers, should be prone to the risks of alcohol and other misadventures that result from not being careful. Addictive drugs, including alcohol, are not universally appealing. A particular drug becomes appealing when a person discovers that the short-term "benefits" of a particular drug become necessary to overcome some facet of or problem with regulating emotions, self-esteem, and relationships. In turn, the pain and distress associated with these vulnerabilities interact with deficits in self-care to make addiction more probable. Addiction problems are less a statement about pleasure seeking, reward, or self-destructiveness than they are about human psychological vulnerabilities.

• 4 •

Self-Medication Hypothesis Research: Study of Affect Regulation and Drug Preference

Jesse J. Suh, Psy.D.

INTRODUCTION*

$\mathcal{A}$lthough the clinical phenomena of the SMH have been captured and further expanded upon by us,[1] numerous scholars and scientists in research settings have extensively investigated the validity of the SMH. In this chapter, we will review empirical evidence that supports the SMH as described throughout this book. Epidemiological and etiological studies citing the prevalence of and risk factors for each class of drugs relevant to the SMH will be considered, as well as laboratory studies establishing the specificity of drug effects. We will then conclude with general recommendations for future SMH research. Because this is not primarily an academic treatise, we will not present an exhaustive litany of all the studies pertaining to the SMH. Rather, we will present a representative sample of pertinent studies. Additionally, many studies have included patients with serious co-occurring psychiatric disorders; findings from these studies may not be fully applicable to the general population.

---

*Although there are many references included in this book, there are a disproportionate number of them in this chapter. We have included them for the benefit of students, scholars, and others who wish to have available the empirical evidence that addicted individuals struggle with regulating emotions and that there is a considerable degree of specificity in the substances drug-dependent people prefer.

DYSREGULATION, SELF-ESTEEM, SELF-CARE, AND RELATIONSHIPS

Most studies supporting or rebutting the SMH have focused on affect dysregulation or the match between psychiatric disorders and substances—so-called pharmacological specificity. Few studies have explored either dysregulation in general, or other self-regulation deficits—self-care, self-esteem, and interpersonal relationships. For example, Wilson et al.[2] found that people with opiate addiction exhibited difficulties in self-regulatory functioning when compared to nonaddicted individuals. Similarly, other researchers noted disturbances in interpersonal relations and affect modulation in opiate-dependent patients[3] and interpersonal difficulties and "self dysfunction" in substance-dependent patients.[4] Given that these clinical studies are retrospective, it may not be possible to establish definitively the self-regulatory issues preceding the onset of the substance use and misuse. Findings from prospective studies, however, indicate that the dysregulation may precede and lead to subsequent substance use. One research group found that in 947 sixteen-year-olds, lower self-esteem was a risk factor for the development of nicotine dependence.[5] Similarly, Shedler and Block[6] examined a group of children from preschool to adolescence and reported that frequent marijuana users, compared to both abstainers and experimenters, had in their childhood and adolescence exhibited not just more emotional distress, but greater interpersonal alienation.

SMH: EMOTIONAL REGULATION AND SUD

Emotional regulation is a vital process that we undergo on a daily basis. We manage negative emotions in response to external stress, reducing our experience of discomfort. Uncomfortable emotions can be managed by changing their intensity or duration.[7] Such is the case when we cope with positive and negative stresses, when we encounter abrupt changes in our lives, or when we simply watch a scary movie.

In children, this regulatory function is an important predictor of their health conditions, including behavioral self-control,[8] depressive symptoms,[9] adjustment problems,[10] social skills,[11] and physical health.[12] Adults who capably manage their emotions are also more likely to demonstrate successful long-term adjustment, better interpersonal functioning, and a higher degree of psychological well-being; however, poor emotional regulators experience greater social anxiety.[13] This self-regulation capacity differentiates depressed adult patients from healthy research participants,[14] and depressed patients who do not respond to treatment from successful treatment responders.[15]

Young people encounter major developmental changes during early adolescence, characterized by the onset of puberty, advancing independence, and social challenges. They need to adapt to and manage new, powerful emotions.[16] Given that substance use problems often begin in early adolescence,[17] a developmental perspective would provide a useful guide to understanding the link between affect regulation and substance use. Negative affect (e.g., anger, fear, frustration),[18] emotional dysregulation,[19] and poor coping techniques[20] have been identified as liability factors for substance abuse in adolescents. When a group of adolescents were studied over a three-year period, the adolescents' negative affect was significantly linked to an increase in substance use.[21] Another study pointed to the important role of emotional dysregulation in substance abuse among incarcerated adolescents with behavioral problems, who used substances to cope with their negative emotions.[22]

Poor affect regulation is a significant risk factor for substance use in adults as well.[23] Adult drug users are more likely to experience difficulties in managing their emotions than nonusers.[24] This relationship between poor affect regulation and substance use is unlikely to result from residual drug effects or drug withdrawal effects, given that the relationship exists in those with an extended period of abstinence.[25] The link between poor affect regulation and substance use involves negative mood states—including depression, anxiety, and anger—that induce drug craving in substance abusers.[26] Additionally, their experience of external stress and negative affect plays a critical role in initiating substance use or relapse.[27] In one interesting recent study, for example, retirees who reported that they had experienced more stressful work environments exhibited higher levels of alcohol consumption during retirement than did those retirees reporting less stressful work environments.[28]

Under laboratory conditions, drug users demonstrated both subjective and physiological abnormalities, showing a significant discrepancy in their ability to regulate emotions from normal samples. When emotionally arousing pictures were presented to a group of abstinent substance abusers, they responded with lower subjective reactions than a normal sample.[29] Additionally, while the healthy subjects demonstrated a significant increase in cardiovascular and neuroendocrine levels, substance abusers showed no such changes in these measures.[30] These demonstrable differences between substance abusers and normal samples indicate that substance abusers respond abnormally when exposed to emotional content. Further, these findings suggest their capacity to manage emotional states may be defective, perhaps underscoring the importance of affect regulation's role in addictions.

SPECIFICITY OF SUBSTANCES

The SMH considers the effects of various drug classes (e.g., stimulants, opiates, and alcohol and sedative-hypnotics) that target the inner states of psychological suffering and personality organization.[31] In chapter 6, we outline the unique qualities of each drug that would appeal to a particular group of substance abusers. Research has shown that drugs are not chosen randomly, but through successive trials substance abusers come upon a substance that alleviates specific affects. After experimenting with numerous classes of substances, most substance abusers prefer a particular class of drugs with similar pharmacological properties,[32] which induce similar psychological effects[33] and meet "central psychological needs."[34]

Opiate Use: Coping with Aggression and Rage

As we describe in chapter 8, painful emotions stemming from traumatic experience can have devastating consequences, including opiate addiction. Opiates, in both natural and synthetic forms, have been widely used medically for their pain-reducing properties.[35] The major specific appeal of opiates involves managing rage and aggression that are linked to an earlier traumatic exposure to painful violence and aggression.[36] Opiate-dependent patients' experience of trauma at various levels elicited aggression, and the patients often had not established the defensive and adaptive psychological mechanisms that would allow them to regulate the rage and aggression.[37] Thus, opiate use functions as an adaptive response that temporarily mutes and attenuates these emotions.[38]

Although traumatic experience is an important vulnerability factor for various substance use disorders,[39] its link to opiate addiction is exceptionally profound. Empirical evidence suggests that opiate users are three times more likely to have a history of childhood abuse,[40] and trauma-related symptoms are associated with greater opiate abuse.[41] The underlying mechanism in opiate addiction involves the appealing qualities of opiate's soothing and calming effect. Given that negative emotions elicit opiate craving,[42] opiate use allows the abusers to modulate painful affects and protects "some addicts from giving direct expression to these destructive impulses."[43] Compared to individuals using other substances, the individuals with heroin use disorders experienced the highest level of trauma severity, indicating a unique association between traumatic experience and opiate addiction. More importantly, individuals who experience higher levels of anger and negativity are more likely to prefer heroin than other substances.[44]

Stimulants and Cocaine: Escaping Depressive State and Emptiness

The acute psychological effects of cocaine use include elevation of mood, increased self-esteem, a decrease in fatigue, and increased energy and productivity.[45] Patients with the need to repel or regulate inner emptiness, boredom, and/or depressive states prefer the powerful effects of cocaine.[46] Cocaine abusers have been shown to suffer from chronic depression, hyperactive symptoms, or bipolar conditions.[47]

The SMH identifies two types of cocaine abusers: "low energy" individuals and "high energy" individuals. "Low energy" cocaine abusers experience chronic feelings of boredom, depression, or fatigue. Various surveys suggest that cocaine use disorders and depressive symptoms are common comorbid conditions,[48] such that individuals with major depression are five times more likely to suffer from cocaine use disorders than those without major depression.[49] Cocaine users are also more likely to show symptoms of depression and psychological discomfort than normal control groups.[50] This connection between depressive moods and symptoms and cocaine addiction is more than coincidental, given that depressed affect is associated with cocaine craving, higher relapse rates, and treatment attrition,[51] and is predictive of stimulant relapse.[52]

Conversely, the "high energy" individuals possess a magnified need for elation and excitement.[53] Many cocaine abusers, for example, attempt to sustain such experiences by leading restless lifestyles (e.g., flight from depression). Previous investigations have identified this subtype of cocaine abusers, who are more energetic, excitement-seeking, and less tolerant of frustration than normal control groups[54] and seek the energizing effects from cocaine use.[55] This need for euphoria appears to be unique for the "high energy" cocaine abusers, in comparison to the users of other substances. For example, individuals who seek exhilarating psychological states and maintain restlessness were more likely to abuse cocaine, whereas this link was not identified in those abusing other substances.[56] In chapter 7, we describe how stimulants can also paradoxically calm and focus individuals with attention deficit hyperactivity disorder (ADHD).

Sedatives and Alcohol: Undoing of Inhibition

Alcohol is a central nervous system depressant with sedating effects[57] that reduces anxiety and produces feelings of relaxation.[58] Individuals who maintain rigid, constricting (i.e., tight) defenses welcome the relaxing effects of alcohol.[59] Alcohol use softens their psychological defenses and allows them release from tense, anxious states. Violent eruptions are commonly seen or heard from alcoholics, whose previously suppressed anger is released upon exposure to alcohol's sedative and dis-inhibiting effects.[60]

Research findings suggest alcohol abusers inhibit and over-contain their experience of emotions, and that alcohol may aid in regulating their affect states. Alcohol abusers present with a high degree of defensiveness[61] and use repression (e.g., prevent themselves from being aware) and denial (e.g., refuse to acknowledge) to inhibit uncomfortable emotions.[62] More strikingly, these characteristics are unique for alcoholic patients. For example, when compared to individuals abusing other drugs, alcoholics had a greater tendency to overcontrol their anger and refrain from acknowledging emotions.[63] One might question whether their emotional inhibition could have resulted from the chronic alcohol use. However, under laboratory conditions, two-week abstinent alcohol abusers also reported further "flattening" emotional experience in their response to graphic, aversive images compared to other drug abusers.[64] Accordingly, we found that an abstinent individual's tendency to inhibit emotions plays a significant role in the individual's preference for alcohol,[65] suggesting that the affect dysregulation manifested in alcoholics may not be a consequence of chronic alcohol abuse.

NEUROBIOLOGICAL EVIDENCE OF THE SMH

As we examine further in chapter 12, recent advances in neuroimaging techniques have allowed researchers to examine unique brain structures and functions associated with psychiatric illnesses, including substance addiction. These tools are used to identify not only the differences between various diagnosed conditions, but to clarify which brain regions are involved in feeling, thinking, and behaving in clinical samples or in healthy controls. This emerging field now offers some clues to the link between affect regulation and addiction.

One specific brain region for emotional experience is the limbic region.[66] Given that there are extensive connections between the prefrontal cortex (PFC) and the limbic areas, which include the amygdala, lateral hypothalamus, and nucleus accumbens, the PFC is thought to be implicated in abnormal emotional functioning and affect dysregulation.[67] Specifically, in normal subjects, voluntary attempts to regulate emotion through the use of emotional coping strategies increased the activation of lateral and medial prefrontal regions, and attenuated amygdala activity.[68] The findings are in agreement with Schore's proposal that dysfunction of the prefrontal and orbitofrontal cortex systems is associated with affective dysregulation.[69]

Recent neuroimaging studies report abnormalities in the frontal-limbic regions for both depression and cocaine dependence. In a comparison to controls, for example, clinically depressed individuals exhibit significantly lower resting regional cerebral blood flow (rCBF) in the prefrontal regions.[70] Cocaine-dependent patients also have the same abnormalities in the regions.[71] One finding pertinent to the SMH involves Sinha et al.'s work with abstinent cocaine-dependent patients.[72] When experiencing stress, cocaine-dependent patients showed lower brain activation in the frontal regions than did healthy controls, suggesting that the patients may possess defective frontal regions, which previously have been linked to emotional dysregulation. Although these results link cocaine addiction to depression (e.g., affect dysregulation) via brain imaging techniques, they do not provide adequate evidence to explain how affect regulation could initiate or maintain substance addiction.

OTHER EVIDENCE SUPPORTING SMH

Numerous psychopharmacological research studies have demonstrated that emotional symptom reduction prevents the likelihood of relapse. We and others have shown that atypical antipsychotic medication treatments, which are often used to stabilize emotional volatility, led to better substance outcome for a prolonged period, reduced psychotic symptoms, and enhanced functioning.[73] More recently, some antidepressants have been found to reduce drug and alcohol use.[74]

NEGATIVE FINDINGS

Although numerous findings support the SMH, others[75] have shown a less than impressive relationship between drug choice and psychological variables. These studies, however, possessed research limitations. First, many of these investigations may have used inappropriate measures to assess psychological dimensions as described in the SMH. The SMH comments on the connection between *emotional symptoms*, and not *psychiatric diagnoses*. For example, Brunette et al. found that there was no correlation between *schizophrenic disorder* severity and substance use in the patients they studied; however, there was a significant correlation between substance use and *depressive symptoms*.[76] Similarly, Henwood and Padgett recently reported that the SMH is empirically supported in studies using relevant constructs to measure subjective, distressful emotions, rather than psychiatric diagnoses or incongruent psychological assessment tools.[77] Additionally, McCarthy et al. found that depression symptoms predicted stimulant use, whereas psychiatric diagnoses did not.[78] Throughout this book we discuss the relationship between psychiatric and substance use disorders. Many, perhaps most, people with affective dysregulation who use self-medication to address this dysregulation do not have a co-occurring psychiatric disorder. Conversely, some well-designed studies have studied populations specifically selected to be emotionally helpful and free of psychopathology. These populations, by definition, are clearly less likely to exhibit emotional dysregulation.

FURTHER RESEARCH

Despite the aforementioned evidence supporting the SMH, further research with better designs and methods is warranted. First, most of the previous SMH investigations were studied retrospectively, and the results are correlational in nature (i.e., they do not confirm cause-effect relationship). For example, a finding of more severe depression symptoms in cocaine-dependent patients than in healthy samples could suggest at least two possibilities: 1) depression symptoms led to cocaine addiction; 2) depression symptoms are consequences of chronic cocaine use. Subsequent research would benefit by examining the relationship between self-regulation deficits—not just emotional dysregulation, but also difficulties in self-esteem, self-care, and relationships and substance addiction prospectively, focusing on the processes leading to substance addiction or relapse. Second, if affect dysregulation is one of the hallmarks of substance addiction, an in-depth study that probes the role of affect regulation in substance addiction could add significantly to our current understanding. Using a behavioral task or an assessment tool to measure affective states (e.g., the constructs of the SMH) could extend previous research findings. Similarly, tools must not focus on conscious mechanisms. The SMH does not imply that people consciously seek out substances that make them feel better; the search and discovery is often more subtle and serendipitous. Furthermore, research tools should not focus on the array of symptoms (e.g., insomnia) that accompany emotional disorders but are not integral to the self-regulation deficits encompassed by SMH.

Studying the self-medication of dysregulated affect is difficult for many reasons. A person might use a substance other than their substance of choice because, for example, it is available and adequately effective. Some may have more than one substance of choice. Likewise, two or more emotions may co-occur. And the nature of the dysregulated affect may change over time, so that the substance of choice could be expected to change. We are reminded of Donald, whom we met in chapter 2, who used a variety of substances to deal with a variety of affective states over time. Finally, using research participants with intoxication or withdrawal symptoms can obscure attempts to measure the underlying emotional states. People must be studied either prior to any substance use, or during periods of significant abstinence.

Most clinicians working with the SUD population would agree that those patients whom we encounter come with various histories of life struggles, painful memories, frustrations, and unmet emotional needs. The SMH, since the beginning of its use in clinical settings three decades ago, meaningfully connects these experiences to substance use and misuse. As illustrated in this chapter, research findings support the clinical phenomena described in the SMH. More importantly, treatments for substance addiction, both psychotherapy and psychopharmacologic therapy, should target ameliorating or improving these psychological characteristics—relieving emotional suffering or making emotional defenses less rigid and restrictive.

Contexts and Models for Understanding Addiction—A Brief Overview

$\mathcal{I}$n a number of ways, we emphasize in this book that addictive drugs are not universally appealing. Cocaine, for example, might produce euphoria in one person and uncomfortable feelings in another. Having said this, one might wonder why some individuals are more susceptible than others to finding addictive drugs appealing. The answer resides in the fact that addictions develop in context. For some the context is predominantly a genetic/biological one, for others it is mainly social or environmental, and for still others a psychological context predominates. It is the interaction of these contexts that determines the development of an addiction.

Modern psychiatric practice at its best embodies this multidimensional view of disorders, including addictive ones, in what is referred to as the "biopsychosocial" perspective. In fact, the official diagnostic compendium for psychiatry, the *Diagnostic and Statistical Manual of Mental Disorders*, fourth edition, text revision[1] defines substance dependence (addiction) as a disorder not just with physiological manifestations—intoxication and withdrawal—but with detrimental effects on the body, psyche, and interpersonal and social worlds of the person with the diagnosis.

In this book we emphasize the psychological context because it is a very important one and has consistently received less attention. In what follows, we will briefly consider the other contexts in which addiction develops and the models we and others adopt to understand and treat it.

CONTEXTS FOR ADDICTIONS

One of the earliest *biological* approaches to studying addiction has been studies examining the role of heredity in the development of alcoholism. The observation that addiction runs in families raises old contentious debates of heredity versus environment in the development of addictive disorders. This is an unfortunate polarization, one of many polarizations concerning substance use disorders (SUDs) but a recurrent and major one, dealing with the causes of addiction. Twin studies have been helpful in delineating the role of both genes and environment, especially studies of identical twins raised separately and apart from their birth parents. If the development of addiction were exclusively genetic, then if one twin develops alcoholism, in 100 percent of cases the other twin should also develop addiction. It turns out that the second twin developed alcoholism about 50 percent of the time.[2] This rate is much higher than in the general population, confirming the role of genetics, but that it is not 100 percent points to the role of environmental factors, both social and psychological. Some of these factors increase the likelihood of addiction, while others protect against it. The role of heredity also raises the question of what is inherited. Is the brain different in its response to alcohol or other addictive drugs, or is it an inherited temperament that makes addictive substances more appealing? Research offers support for both. For example, children of alcoholics may have a serotonin deficiency.[3] Likewise, certain temperaments, such as emotional reactivity, are also associated with the development of SUD.[4] While the genetics underlying SUDs is an area in which we can anticipate enormous growth, one study nicely captures both the integration of genes and environment and an example of what is inherited. Researchers at the National Institute on Alcohol Abuse and Alcoholism (NIAAA) recently reported that girls who suffered childhood sexual abuse were more likely to develop an alcohol disorder if they had a low-activity variant of a gene responsible for an enzyme involved in regulating the body's response to stress rather than a high-activity variant.[5]

In chapter 12 we will review the brain's contribution to the development of addiction. The modern biopsychosocial perspective would suggest that addictive susceptibility is determined by an interaction of these biological factors with the environmental ones that we outline below.

Social and economic contexts or environments and the availability of addictive substances are factors that cannot be ignored in the development of substance use disorders. It is not surprising that the occurrence of SUDs is significantly greater among poor, oppressed minorities, and victims of social upheaval and unrest. Yet the advantages of wealth and privilege do not protect against addictive vulnerability. It is said that time and money are risk factors for addiction. Almost daily the media report stories of substance-driven unusual and troubling behaviors among the rich and famous. And then again, is it by chance that special groups of individuals, such as literary and performing artists, seem to have an unusually greater likelihood of developing addictive problems? One scholar observed that five out of seven literary Nobel laureates were alcoholics.[6] Is it something about writing or about the writer? Although this is a very small sample, this is three to six times the rate of alcoholism in the general population. Clearly, parents and peers can also be either protective or risk factors. For example, the number of household users of substances predicts children's use.[7] And research has consistently shown that substance use or nonuse by friends is strongly correlated with an individual's likelihood of using or not.[8]

Prominent athletes and politicians are not exempt either, as evidenced in public disclosures and literary accounts of misadventures and personal life derailments caused by misuse and dependence on addictive substances. Environments in which hardship, societal disruptions, and community violence occur are a major breeding ground for the development of SUDs. This aspect of addiction could be the focus of a book in and of itself but goes beyond the scope of what we cover in this book. Similarly, the notion that spiritual issues contribute to the perpetuation of addictive suffering has a long history within our field, and is a topic that we cannot substantively explore herein. Psychodynamic psychiatrists, drawing upon the work of the great British psychoanalyst Donald Winnicott, speak of "good enough mothering" as the basis of developing a comfortable and secure sense about oneself.[9] Good enough parenting is virtually impossible in such environments. In violent and socially disrupted childhoods a sense of well-being and inner comfort becomes elusive, leaving its victims chronically discomforted later in adult life. Not surprisingly, such individuals resort to addictive drugs to deal with the unremitting distress such environments instill. As we illustrate throughout this book, suffering is at the heart of addictive disorders, regardless of a person's station in life. Individuals who succumb, in our experience, are almost invariably dealing with major distress, for a wide range of reasons, and that distress is a major factor in their propensity to become addicted. The distress of poverty and environmental hardships heightens addictive vulnerability; the comforts of wealth and privilege do not protect against it.

Another very important context for the development of addictive disorders is a *clinical* one. There is a significantly higher rate of SUDs in persons who suffer with psychiatric disorders. Furthermore, it is worth noting that rates are greater with some psychiatric conditions than others. Bipolar disorder, PTSD, and schizophrenia are associated with an extremely high prevalence of co-occurring SUDs, especially if nicotine addiction is considered. Individuals with these disorders suffer immensely with these conditions and, in our understanding, are attempting to provide some relief by resorting to addictive substances. We elaborate further on these conditions in chapter 7.

MODELS FOR UNDERSTANDING ADDICTIONS

Conditioning models, old and new, have been prominent and popular for studying the addictive experience. Prior to the development of modern neuroimaging techniques, animal models were the main bases for advancing the theory that certain drugs are addictive because of their pleasurable reinforcing properties. Adopting this perspective, researchers emphasized that under experimental conditions rats will randomly self-administer addictive drugs to the exclusion of ingesting water and food to the point of death. As we advance in our knowledge of the neurobiological contributions to addiction, we better understand how endogenous neurotransmitter systems, especially those involving dopamine, have a role in making addictive substances so powerfully reinforcing and pleasurable.[10] Conditioning theory is parsimonious and lends itself well to experimental models, but some conditioning experiments caution us to avoid a reductionistic tendency to explain the complexities of why human beings become addicted. In "The Rat Park Chronicle," investigators found that isolated i.e., caged) rats consumed up to sixteen times more morphine than rats housed in a large colony enclosure, the more natural environment for rats.[11] More recently, investigators demonstrated that when subordinate and dominant macaque monkeys were housed together, subordinate monkeys consumed significantly more cocaine. When the dominant monkeys were housed individually, separately from the subordinate monkeys, however, their rates of cocaine consumption were no different.[12] This suggests that "less happy" animals under restrictive conditions are apt to find addictive drugs more appealing (or to use conditioning terminology, more reinforcing) than might otherwise be the case. Thus, while addictive substances have reinforcing, pleasurable effects, one cannot discount the role of environmental conditions to either mitigate or amplify the reinforcing qualities of the substances.

As noted above, building on the cognitive paradigm, neuroscientists have advanced a *biological* model for the development of addictive disorders. Recently, Home Box Office (HBO) collaborated with the National Institute on Alcohol Abuse and Alcoholism and the National Institute on Drug Abuse (NIDA), to present an ambitious and compelling documentary, *Addictions*. The documentary made clear that learning and conditioning theory continues to loom large in explaining the etiology of addiction. Using modern neuroimaging techniques that track where addictive drugs act in the brain, scientists have focused on how drugs affect the brain. Drawing heavily on conditioning/learning theory, they have helped to explain addiction as a "brain disease" involving "pleasure pathways" in the brain. Again, though, explaining how addictive drugs and behaviors change the brain cannot do justice to either what the drugs do for the person or the major problems with distress and suffering which predispose them to addiction. In fact, the case examples of the individuals interviewed for the documentary, including their descriptions of actions and feelings involved in the course of becoming addicted, made compellingly clear how distressing personal events and unhappiness had been involved when they first became addicted and when they relapsed, as well as how addictions have perpetuated the distress in their lives. Given that many of the experts involved in the documentary are well-established clinicians and researchers who have extensively studied and published findings about painful psychiatric conditions associated with SUDS, it is important that the concepts of "reward" and "pleasure" be balanced by concepts which emphasize the distress-relief aspect of addiction. If there is reward involved in becoming addicted, it seems to us that it is just as reasonable to conclude that the addictive drugs offer the reward of relief from suffering as much as the reward of pleasure itself.

We believe that a *psychological* model, based on psychodynamic theory and guided by modern psychiatric principles, can provide a rich and meaningful pathway for appreciating the nature of the inner psychological terrain which can predispose individuals to addictive illness and relapse. The psychodynamic model derives from psychoanalytic theory and practice. Briefly, this model places focus on psychological structures, content, and processes. Early psychodynamic models, first advanced by Sigmund Freud, proposed a stratified scheme of mental life emphasizing unconscious processes, repression, and instinctual drives. In relation to addiction, not surprisingly, early theories stressed the unconscious and symbolic meanings of addictive substances and behaviors and the influence of destructive and pleasurable drives.[13] While some analysts better appreciated the addicted person's problems with aggression and depression,[14] unfortunately the early emphasis on pleasure seeking and self-destruction continued to predominate throughout the twentieth century and even up to the present time.

Contemporary psychodynamic perspectives have emphasized developmental[15] deficits in psychological structures, feeling life, sense of self, and relationships. In an effort to better explain the nature of the psychological realm, a colleague has made an analogy to a container and its contents.[16] The container refers to psychological makeup (e.g., ego structures and defenses), and the content refers to thoughts (conscious and subconscious), emotions, mental states, and so on. This is a useful metaphor in that addictive drugs affect the nature of the container as well as the nature and intensity of the contents. One of the main functions of the psychological structure (or ego) is to regulate our drives, emotions, thought processes, and behavior. Some individuals are overregulated, others not regulated enough. As we will elaborate further in this book, addictive drugs act upon, change, ameliorate, and/or allow feelings. They do so by direct influence on the feelings and sense of self. In other instances they act by influencing structures and defenses which regulate emotions and sense of self. New directions in psychoanalytic thinking have more recently elaborated on experiences of helplessness, fragmentation, powerlessness, dissociation, and relational difficulties (often played out in the treatment relationship) to explain the bedeviling, repetitious, and seemingly self-destructive aspects of addictions.[17] Respected colleagues in Great Britain have honored the psychodynamic traditions in focusing on psychological vulnerabilities predisposing individuals to SUDs, emphasizing difficulties in feeling modulation, attachment, and narcissistic vulnerability. [18]

A MODIFIED PSYCHODYNAMIC MODEL

In our work we have developed and been guided by a modified psychodynamic model, complemented by a modern psychiatric understanding of addictions. This model provides and stresses a focus that gets at essential aspects of addictive vulnerability. As we have seen in the previous chapter, because individuals susceptible to addiction do not adequately recognize, tolerate, or express their feelings, and because they struggle with problems in self-esteem, relationships, and self-care, we have felt it important to develop and use a modified psychodynamic approach to understand and treat them. The psychodynamic model is in the narrative tradition, or the case-study method. It provides rich information about the nature of peoples' inner psychological life, their adaptation to the external world, and how such factors might predispose them to addiction. In a modified psychodynamic approach a clinician is more friendly, supportive, and interactive than are classical psychoanalytic clinicians. To quote from a previous publication: "This approach provides better access to a patient's inner life and permits a natural unfolding of his or her particular ways of experiencing and expressing emotions. Patients also display characteristic patterns of defense and avoidance that both reveal and disguise the intensity of their suffering, their confusion about their feelings, or the ways in which they are cut off from their feelings. I actively engage with patients and build an alliance that allows them to develop an understanding of how their suffering, defenses, avoidances, and separation from their feelings interact with the specific action of the drugs that they use or prefer. In my experience these modified psychodynamic techniques yield rich and ample clinical data that can explain why substances of abuse can become so compelling in a person's life."[19]

We live in the era of "evidence based" medicine and psychiatry, in which there is major emphasis placed on empirical, scientifically derived data to draw inferences and conclusions about the nature of studied problems and treatments. Unfortunately, many people see this as at odds with other approaches, such as the narrative and case-study methods described here. The former provides important *facts* about addiction, the latter provides invaluable data about the *experience* of addiction. In our opinion, these approaches are not mutually exclusive, but should be employed in a complementary way to explore and understand the factors and experiences which perpetuate and predispose people to addictive suffering.

· 6 ·

Suffering and Self-Medication

BACKGROUND

*W*hen we first wrote about the SMH in 1985,[1] we focused on heroin and cocaine. This was due to the fact that one of us (EJK) had been working in the addiction field for fifteen years and had witnessed and been involved in treating primarily young people who had first succumbed to an epidemic of heroin use in the 1960s and 1970s, and subsequently, to an epidemic of cocaine use in the 1980s. That first paper on the SMH described what we had learned about addiction to those two drugs over that period. Seeing and evaluating so many young people, and unfortunately watching many of them die from these addictions, a number of investigators, us included, felt an urgency to understand why so many were falling victim to these drugs. It was a time of unrest in society, with another unpopular war raging in Vietnam, a vice president and then the president being forced to resign, and political tensions and demonstrations of unimagined proportions. Was it something in society, something in the individual, or some combination of these and other factors that was causing widespread addiction? Some studied alienation, others economic and social inequalities. Scientists were studying neurotransmitters in the brain and the reinforcing properties of addictive drugs in animal models. Psychiatrists initiated diagnostic studies. Psychoanalytic investigators started to consider how developmental and psychodynamic factors might influence addictive behavior, and some of us combined psychiatric and psychodynamic approaches to see what psychological and psychiatric issues might influence the development of addictions. In fact, the then fledgling

National Institute on Drug Abuse (NIDA) convened a series of study groups in which some of us psychiatrists and psychoanalysts were encouraged to collaborate in sharing our emerging understandings of drug dependence.[2]

In Cambridge, Massachusetts, a number of us started to treat and study a large number of people addicted to heroin.* We established a methadone treatment program in 1970, a treatment in which long-acting methadone was used to substitute for the short-acting heroin. This was an approach which, when combined with individual and group counseling, offered hope to individuals for whom there were few if any effective alternative approaches. Similar programs were springing up all over the country and were providing an unparalleled chance to study many addicted individuals in their communities of origin. (Most studies of addicted individuals up until that time had occurred in the federal prison/hospital system in Lexington, Kentucky.) One of us (EJK) was in the midst of psychoanalytic training, but nonetheless had to overcome negative emotional reactions (psychoanalysts refer to such reactions as "countertransference") about "those heroin addicts." In fact, before beginning to work with and treat them, we had to overcome our own prejudices that addicted individuals were menacing people without consciences. Fortunately our psychiatric and psychoanalytic training served both the patients and us, because in taking careful psychiatric and developmental histories, including family and social backgrounds, we very soon began to appreciate how troubled these patients were, especially with regard to their disrupted, often violent, backgrounds, the intense emotions with which they struggled, and their lifelong difficulties with behavioral dysregulation.

Our psychodynamic background caused us to speculate about what purpose opiates might be serving in the lives of the patients dependent on these drugs. Appreciating that opiates are painkillers, we thought that they might be treating psychological pain. Although in general this seemed to be the case, we quickly began to appreciate that a majority of the patients had seemed to struggle throughout their lives, even prior to their becoming addicted, with intense—often unbearable—violent, angry feelings. Patient after patient responded similarly to the question, "What did the heroin do for you when you first used the drug?" Most said it made

---

*For the reader who is interested in additional historical background in the development of these ideas, we refer you to a recently published interview with one of us: E. J. Khantzian, interview by Martin Weegman, "Reflection on Group Therapy," *Journal of Groups in Addiction & Recovery* 1, no. 2 (2006): 15–32.

them "feel normal," or things such as "I felt calm . . . it made my anger go away. . . . I could get going and function." The main feelings that seemed to be countered by the heroin were those associated with anger and related restlessness and agitation. In an intake group we were able to observe how markedly more controlled, less angry, and less verbally abusive they were in their interaction with each other and the leaders as they stabilized on the methadone. Incidentally, with the advent of Suboxone, we have found similar results with that medication. If we had devised an index for obscenities as a measure of angry feelings and tracked them against methadone levels, we would have plotted how as patient methadone levels increased and stabilized there was a corresponding decrease in the use of obscenities and invectives. As an opioid, methadone is just like heroin in its physical and emotional effects, but it is long-acting (up to thirty-six hours) when taken by mouth, and can prevent craving and withdrawal without causing intoxication. Exploring the patients' family and social backgrounds, we found that a disproportionate majority reported exposure to violent and abusive experiences in their growing up years. This initial understanding that individuals resorted to particular drugs to relieve intense, problematic, and intolerable emotions (in the case of heroin addicts, intense rage) represented the budding of the concept of self-medication.

THE EVOLUTION OF AN IDEA

As we indicated, some contemporary psychoanalytic investigators were working, at first independently and then collaboratively, on trying to understand the dynamics of drug addiction problems which were emerging in the second half of the twentieth century. Some stressed the intolerable feelings of rage, hurt, shame, and loneliness that opiate dependent individuals attempted to relieve with opiates;[3] others considered difficulties in recognizing and tolerating painful feelings.[4] A number of researchers introduced terms which suggested that individuals preferred different classes of drugs to deal with emotions that might be particularly difficult for a given individual. "Drug of choice"[5] was a term first introduced by two psychoanalysts working with adolescent substance abusers. "Preferential use of drugs"[6] was a term introduced to distinguish psychological differences between amphetamine and heroin abusers; we adopted the term "self-selection"[7] to differentiate how and why different people were drawn to a particular drug; and two psychologists intensively studying a group of cocaine addicts used the term "drug of commitment"[8] in drawing similar conclusions. It was in the context of these ideas that we spelled out more specifically how addictively vulnerable individuals self-medicate psychological suffering and navigate toward a particular drug to relieve the particular distress with which they suffer.

Why Are Some People More Vulnerable Than Others to SUDs?

Many people suffer with not knowing or tolerating feelings, experience self-doubt, struggle in their relationships, and neglect their self-care. And most people have had some experience with substances or behaviors that hold the potential for being abused. Most people do not become addicted, however. Why? As we have noted previously, the differences between those who become addicted and those who do not are complex, with psychological, social, and biological facets. We emphasize what often gets overlooked, namely that individuals prone to addiction suffer more intensely. We have described heightened difficulties in regulating either their emotions, self-esteem, relationships, or some admixture of these, combined with pervasive self-care deficiencies; these difficulties make for a malignant combination and addiction to substances more probable. In addition to the intensity of distress, people exhibit a range of capacities (i.e., ego capacities) to tolerate emotional distress, a function of growing up environments, temperament, and genes. For example, in subsequent chapters we will discuss how patients with disorders such as post-traumatic stress disorder (PTSD), bipolar illness, schizophrenia, and ADHD have a significantly greater chance of developing a substance use disorder (statisticians would say the odds ratios are much greater). These conditions are associated with extreme distress and diminished capacities to tolerate such distress.

Self-Medication and Drug Preference

The SMH has two aspects to it. The first is that individuals use and become dependent on addictive drugs because they relieve psychological pain and suffering which is unbearable for that individual. The second aspect of the SMH is that there is a considerable degree of specificity with regard to the drug a person comes to favor. In this latter respect, several factors interact to make a particular drug appealing: the chief effect or action of the drug, the personality of the individual (that is, characteristic ways of being and acting which are variously inborn and environmental), inner states of distress or discord, and availability of the substance.[9]

Individuals do not set out to become addicted, and they do not simply choose to become dependent on opiates or stimulants such as cocaine, for example. Rather, in the course of experimenting with various drugs a person discovers that a particular one has a special comforting, alleviating, and/or heightening effect which gives that drug its special appeal. Although many individuals use more than one drug (often in a juggling act to treat the unwanted effects of a previously used drug), when asked, most individuals will volunteer that they prefer one drug. In our experience, the person's expressed drug preference is more often a telltale of particular emotions or psychological states which are problematic or especially painful for that individual. The affinity or preference issue raises the question of how the drugs of abuse are different from each other and how they get to be so desired or preferred. The main classes of drugs upon which people become dependent (i.e., addicted), which we will review here, are opiates, sedatives, and stimulants.

Opiates. Opiates, also referred to as narcotic analgesics, or more commonly "pain killers" are drugs such as heroin, morphine, methadone, Vicodin, Percocet, Percodan, Dilaudid, Oxycontin, and oxycodone. They are best known as powerful painkillers used to alleviate physical pain associated with numerous medical and surgical conditions. Heroin has no approved medical use, but is obtained illegally from dealers, is powerfully addicting, and is used mostly intravenously (when sufficiently potent, it is also snorted). Most other opiates used by dependent individuals are obtained by diversion from medical and pharmaceutical sources. A recently much publicized source is the medicine cabinet of a family member or relative. Some opiates, such as Dilaudid and oxycodone, can be dissolved and injected by intravenous users. Although opiates can calm or quiet a wide range of intense emotions, as addictive drugs they gain their appeal, in our experience, mainly by their powerful calming effects on intense emotions such as rage, violent anger, and the agitation which is often associated with such states.

It should not be surprising then that people who struggle with intense anger and irritability would find the calming and soothing action of opiates seductive and welcome. Intense emotions of any kind are discombobulating and threatening because they disorganize within, but they are also infectious. Aggressive feelings are especially threatening because experiencing them has the unfortunate consequence of provoking or perceiving aggression in others, thus causing a greater sense of jeopardy.

There is also the problem of individuals not being in touch with or aware of their anger and irritability, as we have already indicated, but instead carrying around a vague sense of dysphoria associated with these emotions. As the underlying rage is quieted when they use opiates, the associated dysphoria goes away. Whether the anger is vague and dysphoric or intense and overwhelming, opiates act as a strong antidote. Conditions such as PTSD, bipolar disorders, subtle low-grade forms of bipolar disorders such as hypomania, and certain personality disorders (for example borderline and antisocial) are conditions in which intense anger, irritability, and violent reactions are common. Not surprisingly, such individuals are especially drawn to narcotic pain killers.

Bill, a former celebrity athlete turned rock star, suffered both with PTSD and bipolar mood disorder. He was subject to violent verbal tirades with his wife, and when in public, he was apt to erupt with disdainful, angry reactions when frustrated or rebuffed. He described how heroin was "like putting on a big fuzzy blanket"; he said the anger went away and he could become soft like a teddy bear with his wife, or more readily enjoy the adulation of his fans, no matter the conditions, when he was under the influence of the narcotics.

Sedatives. The drugs in this group are referred to as tranquilizers, on the street as "downers," and in medicine as "sedative-hypnotics." The hyphenated term provides a clue to the appeal of this class of drugs, namely, in low to moderate doses these drugs sedate, calm, and relax; in higher doses they produce sleep and obliterate consciousness. The main drug in this category is alcohol, the most pervasive drug in our culture and many others. Given the widespread availability of alcohol, it is a wonder that there are not more problems with alcohol abuse and addiction. Some argue that the better control of alcohol in Western societies is a function of social sanctions and learning.[10] Although socially acceptable, its excessive and addictive use, along with that of nicotine, causes enormous social costs and medical consequences in society. The two other major drug classes in this category are barbiturates and benzodiazepines. With some minor exceptions, such as the compound Fiorinal, barbiturates such as Phenobarbital and Seconal and barbiturate-like drugs such as Quaaludes, which were widely abused in the 1970s and 1980s, are no longer very prevalent. They have been surpassed by the benzodiazepines which were first introduced in the 1950s as "minor tranquilizers," the first ones being Valium and Librium. Nowadays, Xanax, Klonopin, and Ativan are the more commonly prescribed representatives of this group of drugs. Alcohol and the other sedatives are appealing because they relieve tense, anxious states. Under ordinary circumstances alcohol is used widely as a means to relax and, in social situations, serves as a lubricant for enjoying the company of others. For the more tense and anxious, alcohol and drugs such as the benzodiazepines become more necessary and, consequently, for some their use can become excessive and lead to addiction. The reasons that a person is tense and anxious are multiple and variable. A psychoanalyst citing an unknown source offers the quote, "Our super-ego (or conscience) is that part of ourselves which is soluble in alcohol."[11] The quote explains why, for example, the beginning of a cocktail party is typically subdued and guests are mostly self-conscious; but an hour or so later the volume has increased, there is more buoyancy, and a "who really cares" manner seems to prevail. Those who are very uptight about matters of convention and propriety might excessively resort to alcohol to socialize. This might be one explanation for heavy alcohol use. However, working with patients who have resorted to heavy and addictive amounts of alcohol, we have been impressed with how the tension and anxiety is more extreme and is less often a problem of harsh conscience than the result of extreme discomfort and defensiveness about matters of emotional closeness and dependency. J. R. Moehringer in his memoir, *The Tender Bar*, a book about growing up around the culture of a local tavern, touchingly describes a particular reunion in which alcohol helped him and his estranged father to overcome the guilt and awkwardness about their loving and tender feelings for each other. In this respect, alcohol is not so much a super-ego solvent as it is an ego solvent. Use of alcohol and related drugs under these circumstances allows such individuals brief human contact, warmth, and closeness, which they ordinarily cannot or do not allow, as the following case of Michael demonstrates in a slightly different context:

Michael was a tense and uncomfortable person throughout his adolescent and early adult life. As an engineer he was precise and methodical in his professional and technical dealings with colleagues. In other respects, he considered himself a "born-again isolationist," saying he had a paucity of friends and satisfactory relationships. He described one day in exquisite detail the preparation of a gin martini, including the bouquet of the juniper berries, the crackling of the ice as he poured the alcohol over it, the delight of the burning gin descending into his gut, and then his reaction to the drink as it hit him. He said, "I began to feel free—free to feel. I felt happy, even giddy—unashamed, unpretentious, and uninhibited. I felt that I finally was a member of the human race, 'one of the guys,' an equal." This giddiness was also evident in his face as he was describing the reaction, a demeanor which was in sharp contrast to his usual stern and tense manner.

In contrast to the individuals who become dependent on opiates because defenses are too loose and anger and rage can erupt, tense and anxious individuals such as Michael suffer because their defenses are too tight and do not allow for ordinary needs of human warmth and intimacy. In the former case, opiates are used to shore up defenses and control emotions; in the latter case, sedatives such as alcohol and related drugs are used to loosen defenses and allow feelings.

Stimulants.   High- and low-energy individuals are drawn to the effects of stimulants. Stimulants can boost high-energy people and make them the way they like to be; stimulants can also energize and activate low-energy types and make them feel more likeable. And for persons who suffer with attention deficit hyperactivity disorder (ADHD), stimulants have a calming and focusing effect. There are FDA-approved stimulant medications such as Ritalin and Adderall. On the streets, illegal forms of stimulants such as cocaine and amphetamines have flooded society worldwide over the past three decades. Cocaine can be snorted or used intravenously, as can amphetamines. In a form referred to as "freebase," cocaine is treated with bicarbonate and smoked as "crack" or "rock cocaine." Similarly, amphetamine is converted to crystal methamphetamine and smoked as "crystal meth," "glass," or "ice." The different forms of stimulants determine how rapidly the drugs take effect, the potency of the experience, and the duration of the drug effect.

Stimulants help to overcome feelings of low energy, fatigue, and low self-esteem, problems associated with depression. Because the stimulant counters depression, frustration-tolerance, self-assertion, and self-confidence are improved; feelings of boredom and emptiness are diminished; and a sense of power and control is re-established.[12] When users of cocaine and amphetamines describe the "euphoria" these drugs produce, what they are more likely experiencing is the relief from dysphoria associated with painful depressive reactions and feelings. An individual does not necessarily have to suffer with depression to experience feelings of boredom, low self-esteem, or emptiness and discover how stimulants can counter such bothersome feelings. Stimulants also have a paradoxical effect. Instead of stimulating, they can be calming and focusing for individuals with ADHD. In all of the above situations, individuals wittingly and unwittingly are self-medicating the distress associated with depression, ADHD, and related conditions. It is on this basis that de-energized, discouraged, deflated, disorganized individuals find relief with stimulants, as hyper-energized individuals with bipolar conditions welcome the energizing properties of stimulants to make easier their need to be expansive.

Larry was a successful businessman. Despite his poise and handsome features, he nevertheless felt a deep sense of distrust and lack of confidence about himself. He said that for the most part he had not had any long-term satisfactory relationships with women, despite his attractiveness and success in business. When he was attached to a woman he said he could get lost in the relationship but the slightest frustration could throw the relationship into crisis. He sadly described how, in periods of loneliness and depression, cocaine could help him overcome his self-doubt and feel energized and attractive enough to cruise around and pick up a woman to satisfy his needs.

As we have tried to emphasize thus far, much has been written about how addictive drugs act on the pleasure centers in the brain to produce reward and euphoria, but not enough has been said about the distress which predisposes people to substance use, abuse, and dependence. The enraged find that opiates calm them; the inhibited are released from their uptightness by alcohol; and those who languish with depression are energized and uplifted by stimulants. What too often is missed is the enormous psychological suffering that motivates addictions, and the fact that people resort to their drug of choice because, in the short-term, they can better endure their distress and cope with the internal and external realities that can otherwise feel so unendurable.

Self-Medication, Psychiatric Disorders, and Emotional Pain

*The notion of "self-medication" is one of the most intuitively ap-
pealing theories about drug abuse. According to this hypothesis
drug abuse begins as a partially successful attempt to assuage
painful feelings. This does not mean seeking "pleasure" from the use
of drugs. Rather, individuals predisposed by biological or psychological vulnerabilities find that drug effects corresponding to their
particular problems are powerfully reinforcing.*[1]

The above quote was from an article in the *Journal of the American Medical Association* (JAMA) by the associate editor. It demonstrates that others besides us consider the SMH a good idea. The SMH is useful because
it not only provides a pathway to understanding an important aspect of
what causes addictions, but it also provides a pathway for considering humane and effective treatments for addictive disorders.

The modern understanding of addiction dates back a half century. As
we indicated in chapter 2, there has been a tendency to consider SUD as
a disease. As psychiatrists were increasingly treating drug-dependent individuals in the late 1960s and early 1970s, little attention was paid to co-
occurring disorders or distress. SUDs were seen as independent, primary
diseases responsible for all the devastation in a person's life. Correspond-
ingly, over the next two decades, while the health field understood alcohol's negative effects on all aspects of a person's life, including his or her
mind and body, there was less acknowledgement of the difficulties in people's lives that contributed to the drive to use substances.[2] As the number
of addicted individuals being seen in treatment centers increased, however,
so did the evidence of a disproportionately high incidence of psychiatric

distress and disorders among those patients. Both in the treatment populations and in the national surveys, the evidence was primarily that the
psychiatric disorders had preceded the addictive disorders. Despite these
developments, controversies about causal and sequential relationships between psychiatric disorders and SUDs persisted. One problem has been
that over a good part of the twentieth century standard criteria did not exist to make reliable diagnoses of psychiatric conditions, including SUDs;
as a result, one group observed that estimates of co-occurrence of depression and SUDs among different studies ranged between 3 percent and 98
percent.[3] This made for meaningless comparisons.

Inconsistencies in the estimates of co-occurrence of psychiatric problems have been significantly resolved over the past three decades with the
development of standard criteria for the diagnosis of psychiatric disorders.
The development of the *Diagnostic and Statistical Manual of Mental Disorders* (DSM)[4] has provided reliable diagnoses, and allowed for more
meaningful and consistent comparisons among populations. Using these
diagnostic criteria, numerous studies in treatment populations, including
our own Cambridge Health Alliance survey of opioid-dependent individuals, have demonstrated elevated levels of psychiatric disorders, such as
depression.[5] Over the past two decades large national epidemiological surveys of non-patient populations have also demonstrated a high prevalence
both of psychiatric disorders among people with SUD and of SUDs
among people with psychiatric disorders.[6] For example, one study revealed
that while the lifetime prevalence of psychiatric disorder in the general
population was 48 percent, among alcohol-dependent men it was 78.3
percent, and among alcohol-dependent women it was 86 percent.[7]

So, why make so much of this issue about diagnosing depression and
other psychiatric disorders among people with SUDs? Generally, it has been
well established that when these disorders are diagnosed and treated in
SUD populations, patients have better results. The issue also has specific rel-
evance to the SMH. Psychiatric diagnoses are a reasonably good measure of
distress, especially when standardized, reliable criteria are used. The DSM,
for example, provides an objective categorization of symptoms, which then
becomes the basis of an unbiased diagnosis. This approach has the advantage of providing scientific information which allows comparisons among
different populations of patients. The disadvantage of the DSM approach is
that categorical diagnoses based on a set number of objective criteria can
miss more subtle subjective distress and subsyndromal presentations that do
not rise to the level of a full diagnosis. This has been apparent to us on many
occasions. For example, using a survey that measures depression symptoms,

we interviewed men who were admitted to a residential addictions program and found that even relatively mild depression symptoms, symptoms that would not qualify somebody for a DSM diagnosis, predicted the likelihood that these men would leave treatment prematurely.[8]

A recent advance in taking the subjective, subtle distress into account has been the development of the *Psychodynamic Diagnostic Manual* (PDM)[9] which compliments the DSM-IV-TR by placing much more emphasis on the subjective internal emotional and cognitive experiences associated with each diagnostic category. In our opinion, the combination of the two approaches embodied in the DSM and the PDM can best unravel the relationships between psychiatric and psychological distress and the development and maintenance of SUDs.

Much attention within the addictions field has been paid to which disorder, SUD or psychiatric, manifests first. If the SUD has the earlier onset, then support would seem to diminish for a self-medication perspective. If, on the other hand, the onset of the psychiatric disorder predates the onset of the addictive disorder, then one could argue that this is at least circumstantial evidence of causality—that is, that the psychiatric disorder is at the root of distress that individuals are self-medicating with their drug of choice, and that successful treatment of this disorder should affect patterns and amounts of addictive drug use. Of course, whatever the order of appearance, integrated treatment of both is crucial, as we will see in chapter 13. Also, whatever the order of appearance, it is possible that these disorders exist independently of each other, and that neither affects the onset of the other. And it is important to remember that the lifestyle of addiction, by its nature, predisposes individuals to realities such as loss, depression, and trauma, which further reinforces the addiction.

Over the past two decades, epidemiological and clinical studies have indicated that more often, the onset of the psychiatric disorder predates the onset of the SUD. For example, in one study of almost three hundred cocaine abusers, 68 percent of those with an anxiety disorder and 99 percent of those with attention deficit disorder reported that the psychiatric disorder had preceded the cocaine use.[10] In a large study of the United States' population, researchers found that among both men and women with an alcohol disorder and co-occurring psychiatric disorders, at least one psychiatric disorder began at an earlier age than the alcohol disorder in most cases.[11] In examining the results from this same general population study, our colleague Howard Shaffer found that for most people with cocaine dependence and a comorbid psychiatric disorder, the latter preceded the onset of *any* cocaine use.[12]

In the remainder of this chapter we will discuss how the emotional pain associated with mood disorders, schizophrenia, anxiety disorders, and ADHD conspire with addictive substances to make misuse of and dependence on them more likely, in what is referred to as the "dually diagnosed patient." The co-occurrence of post-traumatic stress disorders (PTSD) and SUDs will be reviewed separately in the next chapter.

MAJOR DEPRESSION AND BIPOLAR DISORDER*

Recent studies offer insight into the relationship between depression and SUDs. For example, in a study of youths aged twelve to seventeen who had not previously used alcohol, those who experienced a major depressive episode in the past year were twice as likely to have initiated alcohol use in the past year as those who had not experienced a depressive episode.[13] Similarly, another study found an association between major depression and binge drinking among women, suggesting that women use alcohol to deal with the depression.[14] And in a twenty-one-year longitudinal study, researchers following a birth cohort of 1,265 children found that individuals with depression in adolescence were at significantly greater risk of later SUD.[15]

Exploring how depression relates to SUDs shows why maintaining a focus on the subjective aspects of the condition is important. Depression, beyond the basic aspect of a gloomy outlook, poor self-esteem, and guilt, has many faces. Some experience depression wherein anger predominates; in other cases, agitation, anxiety, or physical and emotional sluggishness are the most prominent features. Substances of abuse and their actions interact with a range of states and feelings that can be associated with depression. For example, *analgesic opiates* calm, mute, and contain angry, rageful emotions.

Bipolar disorder is the psychiatric disorder that demonstrates the highest prevalence of addictive disorders. Not surprisingly, SUDs are especially associated with the more difficult-to-treat subtypes of bipolar disorder, such as dysphoric mania.[16] Furthermore, individuals with this disorder report bipolar symptoms as the reason for using substances. For

---

*The following sections on depression, anxiety, and schizophrenia are based on a previously published article: E. J. Khantzian, "The Self-Medication Hypothesis Revisited: The Dually Diagnosed Patient," *Primary Psychiatry* 10 (2003): 47–54.

example, in a recent study, forty-two[17] of forty-five (93.3%) bipolar patients with SUD reported that they initiated substance use because of a bipolar symptom, including depression (77.8%) and irritability (57.8%). And, of note, most (66.7%) felt that their bipolar symptoms improved with the substance use.

Depressant drugs (alcohol, benzodiazepines, barbiturates), the lead candidate of which is alcohol, have a twofold action depending on dose. In high or obliterating doses, alcohol attenuates or lessens a range of intense feelings, including agitation, anger, and irritability, feelings often accompanying depression. In low to moderate (i.e., releasing) doses, depressants can relieve states of anxiety or tension associated with depression. It is worth inserting here that alcohol is not a good antidepressant, but rather in low to moderate doses it can soften or dissolve the rigid defenses against closeness in certain individuals that can be associated with depression (see chapter 6 on how this action helps such individuals to feel better, in the short term). *Stimulant drugs* are activating and energizing and most often are experienced as a magical elixir countering the debilitating anhedonia of depression (i.e., the inability to experience pleasure). They also are welcomed by many hypomanic individuals as augmenting drugs that heighten their expansive, high mood.

Interestingly, some studies support this notion that patients continue to use substances because of their specific effects on the patients' moods. For example, one study demonstrated that bipolar patients drank alcohol when manic, and used cocaine when depressed.[18] Another investigator has noted that bipolar patients will use stimulants to accentuate hypomania.[19] And in a large epidemiological study, mania was strongly associated with sedatives, tranquilizers, and opiates, all of which tend to be calming to the central nervous system.[20]

ANXIETY DISORDERS

As with so many psychiatric disorders, anxiety disorders are more often related or linked to the personality of the person who suffers them. Individuals subject to anxiety disorders tend to be tense, "tightly wrapped," isolative, and cut off from others. *Depressants* in low to moderate doses act as unwrapping and connecting agents, an effect that helps people to feel and express their feelings and to connect to others when they ordinarily cannot do so. In more severe cases of anxiety disorders, such as panic reactions, higher doses of alcohol are employed to calm the terror such states can produce. As one patient put it, "I drink twelve beers to kill the panic, or two to three to preempt it." *Stimulants* can have a similar effect but on a different basis; that is, the activating properties of a drug like cocaine can help such individuals break through their inhibitions. Presumably *opiates'* general muting action can quiet anxiety, but based on clinical experience, most individuals do not become hooked on opiates on this basis.

Recent studies have lent support to the observation that people with anxiety disorders will use substances to make the anxiety more tolerable. In one study comparing people with and without social anxiety, the investigators found that both groups used alcohol to relieve social discomfort, but that the people with the social anxiety disorder used it more often, both in anticipation of social situations and during them, avoided social situations where alcohol was not available, and experienced greater relief from anxiety.[21] Similarly, in a very large survey of the United States' population, researchers found that almost 22 percent of people with an anxiety disorder reported that they self-medicated with alcohol and drugs. Generalized anxiety disorder had the highest self-medication rate, almost 36 percent.[22] And in a large epidemiological study cited above, panic disorder was also strongly associated with the central nervous system calming agents—sedatives, tranquilizers, and opiates.[23]

SCHIZOPHRENIC DISORDERS

Perhaps there are two aspects of schizophrenia that are not well appreciated beyond professional circles. In reviewing the appeal of various addictive drugs for patients who suffer with schizophrenic disorders, it is important to distinguish between positive and negative symptoms associated with schizophrenia:

Table 7.1.   Positive and Negative Symptoms of Schizophrenia

Positive Symptoms	Negative Symptoms
Delusions	Alogia (paucity of words)
Hallucinations	Affective flattening (emotional dulling)
Disorganized speech	Anhedonia (inability to feel pleasure)
Disorganized or	Asociality (inability to socialize)
Catatonic behavior	Avolition/Apathy (anergia)
	Attentional impairments

Positive symptoms presumably would be attenuated by *analgesic opiates* because of their calming and organizing action, especially with the accompanying rage and aggression associated with schizophrenia. However, with some rare exceptions where heroin is readily and easily available, schizophrenic patients are unable to obtain opiates because their disorganized condition in most instances makes them unable to negotiate the hazards to obtain opiates. Then again, *alcohol* is readily attainable by such patients, and is extensively abused by schizophrenic patients. In obliterating doses, alcohol attenuates the voices, delusions, agitation, and anger which schizophrenic patients experience. As one patient put it, "When I drink I can dismiss them [the voices] and not be so distressed by them."

It probably is the case that negative symptoms are significantly more important in determining reliance on addictive substances among schizophrenic patients than positive symptoms, especially if dependence on nicotine is taken into account. In part this is because negative symptoms are a prominent and residual aftermath of the more acute phase of schizophrenia when the patient is apt to be too disorganized to obtain or use substances of abuse. There is also enormous suffering associated with negative symptoms, often not immediately apparent, that causes patients to resort to substances for relief, even if the relief is only transient.

> A case example of a particularly taciturn patient, Barry, a 48-year-old man with chronic schizophrenia, stands out. He insisted that he did not belong in the hospital. With a little prompting he said that he was an inhibited man who felt uncomfortable with people. He explained that drinking alcohol allowed him to be more talkative and involved. The clinical team members corroborated this by describing his demeanor and interaction just after he returned—still intoxicated—after an escape. He was characterized as being unusually "affable, warm, friendly, and talkative." He agreed that alcohol was one of the few ways in which he came alive and felt normal among other human beings. He said, "I am inhibited, I don't say much, and I keep to myself if I am not drinking."[24]

There is a disproportionate abuse of *stimulants* among patients suffering with schizophrenia. This might be surprising given the tendency of stimulants to cause psychosis. But in fact there is evidence indicating that schizophrenic patients find relief from their anhedonia and other negative symptoms through the activating properties of stimulants, including nicotine. If still taking their antipsychotic medications, they experience the uplifting benefit of the stimulants without necessarily developing psychotic reactions. Similarly, low to moderate doses of *alcohol* counter the negative symptoms of asociality in such patients, as Barry's case exemplifies. We published case material showing that when negative symptoms of patients, especially their inability to express their feelings and socialize, were relieved by a modern antipsychotic (clozapine), there was a corresponding decrease in patients' reversion to alcohol use.[25]

It is worth mentioning that some substances, such as marijuana, can cause psychotic symptoms such as delusions and hallucinations. The most current evidence suggests that marijuana causes these symptoms in people with an underlying vulnerability to psychotic symptoms.[26] Recent literature also suggests that schizophrenic people may use substances to self-medicate distressful symptoms. For example, depressive symptoms among schizophrenic people were correlated with substance use.[27] And other investigators found that their schizophrenic patients with SUDs used drugs to relax and increase emotions.[28]

ATTENTION DEFICIT HYPERACTIVITY DISORDER

Aside from the well-known problems of attentional difficulties, hyperactivity, and distractibility associated with attention deficit hyperactivity disorder (ADHD), there are significant problems with emotional stability, irritability, anxiety, and depressive symptomotology associated with this condition. These problems cause significant dysfunction in daily life, including work and personal relationships, contributing to problems with self-esteem and a sense of personal efficacy. Many individuals with ADHD learn to compensate and become high achievers and enjoy much success; but many more are unhappy because of this handicap. Furthermore, full-blown mood and anxiety disorders have been documented in numerous studies to co-occur with ADHD.[29] Clearly, ADHD is a risk factor for the development of SUD in late adolescence and adulthood.

Dr. Ned Hallowell, a pioneer in raising awareness of ADHD in adolescents and adults, and author of *Driven to Distraction*, informs us that young people and adults with ADHD love marijuana.[30] We would consider that the dual effects of stimulation and sedation of marijuana help calm and focus people with ADHD, thus its appeal to such individuals. Significantly, patients with ADHD respond to stimulants with a paradoxical calmness and focus. This is the good news and the bad news. It is the good news in that when diagnosed and treated early in adolescents (and of course in adults as well), much of the dysfunction and unhappiness associated with ADHD is circumvented. In fact, some of the most prominent investigators/clinicians treating adolescents with ADHD have produced important findings; they showed that such patients treated with stimulants are much less likely to develop SUDs, including nicotine dependence, than are comparable adolescents not treated with stimulants.[31]

The bad news is that many with ADHD who are not patients also wittingly and unwittingly discover the short-term advantages in coping with life with the stimulating effects of cocaine and amphetamines. In reconstructing such patients' experiences succumbing to stimulant dependence, they report a calming effect and better concentration. As opposed to their peers who "rev up" with cocaine, for example, they describe "zoning down" and calming down with the stimulant. In fact, we have described our encounters with patients who appeared to be self-medicating ADHD-related symptoms with cocaine, and when treated with Ritalin had resolution of ADHD symptoms without experiencing drug relapse.[32] With uncontrolled, nonmedical conditions, most of the time use escalates; with cocaine, for example, use progresses from snorting to more dangerous routes of use such as shooting up intravenously or smoking it ("freebasing"). Cocaine and amphetamine addiction, in our experience, can be one of the most rapidly progressing and debilitating disorders. The natural progression to the most severe consequences can occur over a matter of months, as compared to alcohol dependence, which can span years to decades before the most severe complications develop.

THE REMARKABLE CASE OF BETSY

Betsy came into treatment for her cocaine dependence in 1982. She was thirty-four years old at that time. When seen initially she was in severe withdrawal, suffering with marked depression, totally unable to sleep, devoid of interest in her surrounds, immobile, and with little or no appetite. Her history and treatment response were extraordinary. She claimed that as an adolescent she began to use amphetamines, obtained through a "diet doctor," presumably to help her control weight gain (a period when this drug was legal for that purpose). She reported that amphetamines ("speed") were remarkably uplifting drugs for her in that she was able to do her homework, felt better about herself, and functioned better than she ever had previously. She rapidly increased the amounts and frequency of use, obtaining it legally and illegally in whatever way she could. When the speed became more difficult to obtain, and cocaine became more available, she switched to cocaine, at first snorting and then after several years escalating to intravenous use. The amount of cocaine increased dramatically to the point where she was using a quarter of a million dollars' worth a year. This was possible because a close friend was high in the cocaine distribution chain—Betsy purchased enough both to satisfy her habit and to sell, which gave her enough money to afford her supply.

After her first appointment, agitated and discouraged, she despaired that any help was forthcoming. As a result, she missed her next appointment, during which she went on another "cocaine run." It lasted over a week, but with the firm insistence of her mother and a friend she conceded to another visit. On this visit she had all the worst signs and symptoms of cocaine toxicity: She was grimacing, literally gnashing and grinding her teeth, and digging at imagined bugs crawling under her skin (referred to as "tactile hallucination"); she was dirty, uncombed, and disheveled. Piecing together her past history, with the help of her mother, the doctor ascertained that she suffered with ADHD and that she had unconsciously self-medicated herself for it. Unfortunately, as so often happens, she had rapidly become addicted. The doctor decided to treat her with Ritalin, a treatment which to the doctor's knowledge had not been tried; that is to treat a person addicted to cocaine with a medically approved stimulant, but in this case not to support the addiction but to treat the underlying condition. The short and remarkable version of this case was that she immediately and beneficially responded to the Ritalin medication. After her visit she took her prescribed medication and took a "normal nap" (usually cocaine addicts "crash" into a coma-like sleep lasting up to several days and then are unable to sleep). When she checked in by phone with the doctor later that day as asked, she said she had just awoken from the nap and did not feel like she had any drug in her, but now felt she had a choice whether to use or not. This patient has been followed regularly for twenty-five years and has had no recurrence of her dependence on cocaine. She has resumed a normal family life and started to work, after years of unemployability, which she continues up to the present. This case was reported in the psychiatric literature as an extreme case with marked improvement with Ritalin.[33] *The encouraging results of this case were essentially ignored for almost two decades, but in the context of a methamphetamine epidemic over the past decade and a half, pioneering investigators have begun to scientifically demonstrate the utility and benefit, in some cases, of medically substituting approved stimulants for those used illegally by individuals addicted to cocaine and amphetamines.*[34]

✍

From our perspective Betsy's case was a superb example of how a good theory can guide treatment and result in a remarkable outcome. The suffering associated with SUDs might or might not be associated with co-occurring psychiatric disorders as was the case with Betsy. Beyond the distress of the psychiatric conditions associated with SUDs which we have elaborated upon, for some it is discovering an escape from persistent irritability or anger through the mellowing effect of an opiate and then finding that the hook is set. For others inertia is overcome by cocaine, which allows them to join and enjoy a party. The tense and anxious realize that a drink or two is necessary to ask for the elusive date, but then more and more of it is required to maintain contact, and gradually it becomes physically and emotionally necessary because one is addicted. If any of these life challenges were hard initially, they are now compounded because the very emotions they could not tolerate to begin with are dreadfully amplified as a consequence of the dependence and the feelings which emerge upon withdrawal. The vicious cycle of addiction is established. This condition is not one of moral failure, but those who succumb to these disorders and those who witness them judge themselves and are judged harshly and mercilessly. The SMH is a hopeful and forgiving means to better understand and treat a disorder that can be so elusive and destructive. Such a perspective can then allow for seeing such behavior as an attempt to solve a problem, albeit misguided, rather than cause one, which it invariably does.

Trauma and the
Self-Medication Hypothesis

$\mathcal{A}$s we have emphasized throughout this book, suffering and psychological distress are at the root of addictive disorders. Nowhere is this more evident than with individuals who have experienced major trauma and succumbed to SUDs. A recent and authoritative book on SUDs and posttraumatic stress disorder (PTSD)[1] makes the point that the majority of patients follow a pattern in which the development of PTSD preceded the development of the SUD and that treating both conditions could improve the outcome for both disorders. These authorities also indicate that individuals who experience PTSD are four times more likely to succumb to SUDs than are individuals who have not experienced PTSD. Furthermore, PTSD is associated with poorer prognostic features, such as earlier initiation of drug use, more severe drug use, and poorer treatment adherence.[2]

As we will explore in this chapter, PTSD has associated with it characteristic enduring and unrelenting torment. As we mentioned in chapter 1, for some the trauma and suffering date back to early development when, unimaginably, they were subjugated to either physical, sexual, or psychological abuse or some combination of these, leaving indelible life-long effects. For others the trauma occurs later in life; such is the case with combat veterans, rape victims, people injured in violent accidents, and victims of terrorist attacks and natural disasters such as Hurricane Katrina. It is no surprise, for example, that in the wake of 9/11 New Yorkers exposed to the attack on the World Trade Center exhibited increased binge drinking and alcohol dependence.[3] Furthermore, as we mentioned in the previous chapter, the addiction lifestyle itself contributes to an ongoing pattern of trauma. In chapter 9 we elaborate on the many painful consequences of addiction and how and why individuals perpetuate their suffering.

Our esteemed Cambridge Health Alliance colleague and pioneer in trauma research and treatment, Dr. Judith Herman, has said: "Traumatic events overwhelm the ordinary systems of care that give people a sense of control, connection, and meaning."[4] We have observed that PTSD is a disorder which disrupts essential aspects of human life—feelings, self-esteem, relationships and self-care. As we discussed in chapter 3, these facets of life are fundamental to the capacity for self-regulation. Understanding how and why PTSD victims with SUDs suffer so much, and why substances of abuse become so compelling, is probably best understood by examining how disrupted these capacities become when vulnerable individuals experience major trauma. The suffering becomes pervasive and persistent, and does not readily yield or recede with time. Fortunately, or unfortunately, the suffering and symptoms of PTSD temporarily yield to the effects of substances of abuse and thus they run the risk of becoming addictive.

In chapter 12, we will examine more closely the interplay between neurobiology and psychology as it pertains to the development of addictive disorders. PTSD offers an example of this interplay. Research is suggesting that childhood trauma can cause persistent dysregulation of the body's stress response systems, which leads to negative affect symptoms. It is not too much of a leap to understand the observed increased use of alcohol and drugs as an attempt to self-medicate this distress. A vicious cycle is set up as the substance use further dysregulates the stress system, and we observe out-of-control behavior.[5]

TRAUMA, SUFFERING, AND SUBSTANCE DEPENDENCE—A CASE VIGNETTE

A colleague has persuasively captured the nature of the persistent and unyielding suffering associated with PTSD, "a fate worse than death—endless suffering."[6] A patient, seen by one of us (EJK), embodied this painful dilemma in an extraordinary way.

Henrietta[7] was a woman in her late twenties who had suffered childhood trauma and who through much of her short adult life had persistently displayed all of the painful features associated with it. Among her many bodily dysfunctions and complaints were severe and unrelenting headaches which became complicated by the development of a physical and psychological dependence on analgesic opiates. She also experienced emotional anesthetic withdrawal under her bedcovers for days at a time, alternating with extended tirades of rage directed at family or anyone else who came within the orbit of her care. In the last years of her life, the realization that as a young child she had been repeatedly violated sexually by her grandfather had only heightened her volatility and seething anger. There were two occasions to witness her rage and volatility while she was being evaluated. The first was when advice was sought on the suitability of utilizing methadone both for headache relief and as a means to ameliorate her disabling emotional instability. The initial contact with her helped the consultant to appreciate her "endless suffering" firsthand when reviewing her history and symptomology. Serendipitously, on her second visit, there was a chance to indirectly observe the unsettling nature, for herself and others, of her intense anger and volatility when the consultant came upon her in the parking area outside of his office screaming at her mother, literally for the community to hear, over some real or imagined outrage she was experiencing.

Several weeks after the last appointment the consultant was shocked, yet not totally surprised, when her mother called to inform him that she had found Henrietta dead a few hours earlier, lying face down in her crumpled-up bedcovers, having apparently smothered to death. Her mother explained that her daughter had probably oversedated herself, given her penchant to self-medicate her distress, and presumed her death was inadvertent. She wanted to emphasize this point because there were no recent suicidal threats, and she had been more buoyant recently because of a relationship with a new boyfriend. In addition, she was positively anticipating treatment with a new therapist. As the distressing conversation with Henrietta's mother went on, what became more daunting for the consultant was the mother's insistence that an autopsy not be performed on her daughter. She persisted in asking that whatever possible influence be exercised to prevent a likely mandatory autopsy by the medical examiner. The mother explained that her daughter had an ongoing premonition of an early death, dreading that even in death she would be violated. Henrietta had expressed the wish that she never "be cut open" under such circumstances. At first the consultant thought her mother's almost sole concern and preoccupation with the autopsy so soon after discovering Henrietta's body represented some misunderstanding between herself and her daughter. The consultant subsequently concluded that this consideration probably was not the main one for Henrietta's mother. In fact, the real meaning of Henrietta's and her mother's concern became clearer to him the next day. Namely, he recalled the quote, "a fate worse than death—endless suffering." It became clearer that Henrietta's mother was the transmitter of what Henrietta knew and felt, that is, a much deeper and more pervasive fear and terror. It was so great, in fact, that she believed her suffering to be endless and that even in death she would be violated. As a footnote to her case, it is also worth mentioning the importance of opiates in her life. They were one of the few agents that ameliorated the other dominating emotion that constantly threatened to overwhelm her, namely her rage. We will elaborate below on this appeal of opiates.

THE EXPERIENCE OF PTSD

As we discussed in chapter 7, the development of the *Diagnostic and Statistical Manual* (DSM-IV) has allowed the development of objective criteria for the diagnosis of psychiatric disorders. This includes criteria for PTSD. The following is a summary of the DSM-IV symptoms for PTSD:

- A person experiences an event in which the trauma is experienced as a threat to his or her life or to the physical sense of well-being of self or others, resulting in extreme fear, helplessness, or horror.
- The traumatic event is reexperienced as intrusions of disturbing images, nightmares, and recurrent pain when cues remind them of the trauma.
- The person persistently avoids reminders of the trauma and experiences numbing of general reactions.
- There are continuing symptoms of increased arousal, such as difficulty falling asleep, irritability, and angry reactions.
- Symptoms persist beyond a month.
- The trauma causes major distress or disability in relationships, work, and other important areas of functioning.

In our experience extreme emotions, especially feelings of anger and rage, alternating with emotional numbing, increased arousal, and erratic behavior are the predominant reactions which predispose affected individuals to find relief in the effects of addictive substances. Certainly, Henrietta endured these extremes of emotions and behavior, so much so that she imagined them to extend for her into death.

PTSD, SELF-REGULATION, AND ADDICTIVE DRUGS

Depressants

More than anything, PTSD causes major disturbances in the capacity for self-regulation. Beyond disrupted and distorted emotions, trauma causes major damage to people's self-esteem and interpersonal relationships. They struggle with a lifelong sense of guilt and shame as if they did something wrong. And not inconsequentially, their relationships are fraught with distrust and the inability to satisfactorily connect with others. It is understandable then that the effects of a moderate amount of alcohol might briefly allow a person with traumatic childhood injuries, who has learned self-protective restraint and reserve, to welcome and need the softening effects of alcohol.

Andrea, an accomplished lawyer, had been repeatedly sexually abused by an older brother and his friends starting at 12 years old. She was cynical about her friends, especially her doctor friends, and despite her good standing as a respected professional she had the reputation of being cold and aloof. And, despite her attractiveness and accomplishments, a permanent relationship with a man had eluded her, although she wished for one. She described how she had discovered that alcohol could predictably help her to regulate relationships. She indicated it helped to defrost her reserve and connect to her companions. She reported that enjoying the company of others was almost impossible without the lubricating effects of alcohol, so much so that she had become hopelessly addicted and required detoxification in a rehabilitation center.

Stimulants

For others the problems of low self-worth and the sense of emptiness resulting from PTSD are dramatically and powerfully overcome by the energizing and activating properties of stimulants such as cocaine or crystal methamphetamine.

Jeff described how his ordinarily lethargic and unconfident way of being was radically altered when he snorted cocaine for the first time. Sadly, he had endured repeated unprovoked beatings at the hands of his father from an early age. He described himself as chronically tormented by feelings of self-doubt and low self-esteem most of his life, and was subject to recurrent bouts of self-recrimination and misgivings in his social and work interactions. Other researchers have described traumatized people as "living life fearfully" and having "a restricted world."[8] *Despite his troubled background, he was a successful engineer who had overcome his traumatic childhood to realize his achievements. He reported this tragic history in a way that was so detached and unemotional that it was chilling to the interviewer.*

He said that a group of associates had introduced him to cocaine when he was mildly intoxicated at a company Christmas party. After reluctantly agreeing to snort a few lines of cocaine he said that he suddenly felt less than his usual "nerdlike" self; he indicated that he was able to experience unfamiliar confidence and energy to the point that he danced all night with women whom he had not dared approach previously. Remorsefully, he described how he subsequently became obsessed with obtaining and using more and more of the cocaine, to the point where he spent a small fortune on the drug, became progressively more dysfunctional at work, and ultimately lost his job.

Narcotic (Opiate) Drugs

As we have previously reviewed, narcotic pain killers are drugs that can have a dramatic dampening effect on angry and rageful feelings. They can make a person who feels unhinged by irritable and agitated feelings suddenly feel calm and mellow. Recurrent feelings of violence and rage are one of the most prominent hallmarks for those who have suffered traumatic life experiences. We have worked with intravenous heroin-addicted individuals, adolescents in their mid to late teens who have become addicted to medically prescribed oxycodone, and physicians who self-medicate their troubled and intense emotions with Percocet, another prescribed narcotic drug. Strikingly, regardless of their background, they describe how the drug made them feel normal, calm, or mellow. Working with many individuals who have experienced major psychological trauma, we have been impressed with how their feelings of intolerable rage and violent emotions, deriving from traumatic experiences and memories, were markedly alleviated by the effects of narcotic painkillers.

Paul, an accomplished and distinguished oral surgeon, described a long-standing inner sense of discomfort and angry agitation. He had a vague inkling that his irritability originated from early childhood, when his mother had been subject to violent outbursts of verbal and physical attacks, probably secondary to a disruptive bipolar mood disorder. Although he had a reputation as a poised and confident surgeon, Paul experienced periods of violent anger and irritability with his wife and children. Acknowledging how damaging this was for his fam-

ily, he also emphasized how disturbing and disorganizing (dysphoric) it was for him as well. He sheepishly related how he had discovered the containing and calming action of narcotics. He said, "It was like from heaven, like love at first sight. . . . I could feel at peace, more loving . . . more loveable." In addition to the ameliorating effect on his emotions and behavior, he was also aware how he could calm down enough to do his paperwork brought home from work. Unfortunately, the romance with the narcotics was so consuming that his medical license was suspended for illegally prescribing the drugs for himself. Fortunately with intensive rehabilitation he was able to resume practice after a long course of treatment and protracted supervised abstinence from the drugs.

Addictive drugs are not universally appealing. But they can be more appealing for those who have suffered major traumatic experiences. Such trauma causes the brains and the minds of its victims to react differently to addictive substances. The biology and psychology of such experiences triggers a unique and exaggerated sensation of relief or even pleasure for PTSD victims, whereas otherwise the response to addictive drugs might be one of indifference or even aversion.

Henrietta, Andrea, Jeff, and Paul suffered one of the most unfortunate fates experienced by humans, a traumatic assault on their physical and emotional being. As we can see, the effects were profound and enduring, producing overwhelming and intolerable feelings or emotional blunting, and psychological constriction and defensiveness about human contact. Addictive drugs obtain their power to captivate—if not take prisoners of—such individuals because in the short-term the drugs relieve them from their intolerable distress, or remove them from the imprisoning psychological defenses which they impose on themselves for protection. In various instances it can be the releasing or drowning effects of alcohol, depending on the dose, or the uplifting and mobilizing action of stimulants, and/or the smoothing or dampening effects of opiates on rage and agitation that can be so disorganizing. Unfortunately, the attempts at self-correction are short-lived and all too often replaced by the suffering associated with addiction. Though not intended, addictions take on a painful repetitive and alternating pattern of relief and suffering that becomes compelling and puzzling in its own right—the focus of the next chapter.

· 9 ·

Addiction and the Perpetuation
of Suffering*

*Man is sometimes extraordinarily, passionately, in love with suf-
fering.*

Fyodor Dostoyevsky

$\mathcal{A}$nyone who experiences, witnesses, or treats addiction invariably becomes aware of how devastatingly damaging and painful a condition it is.
Whether it is unwanted side effects, aftereffects, or toxic or withdrawal reactions, the pain and distress of addictive involvement is invariable. Cri-
tiquing the self-medication hypothesis, one may ask why, if people are
self-medicating psychological pain for relief, they continue to perpetuate
or even heighten their pain? The answer is complex. In part, addicted individuals indicate a willingness to endure the pain caused by the use and
dependence upon addictive substances in order to achieve the relief and
coping, albeit short-lived, the substances allow. Neuroscientists argue that
the painful relapses associated with addiction can be simply explained by
the biological distress of acute and protracted withdrawal, which compels
an individual to resort to their drug of choice despite knowing there will
be painful aftereffects and consequences. Old[1] and more recent[2] theories
speculate that the painful, recurrent, self-destructive aspects of addiction
are the result of aggressive instincts and impulses turned on the self to
atone for the guilt such powerful emotions engender. Other contemporary
theorists suggest that the painful repetitions associated with addictions are

---

*This chapter is based in part on a previous publication: E. J. Khantzian and A. Wilson, "Substance
Abuse, Repetition and the Nature of Addictive Suffering," in *Hierarchical Conceptions in Psychoanalysis*, ed. A. Wilson and J. E. Gedo, 263–83 (New York: Guilford Press, 1993).

an attempt to overcome vague and distressing traumatic emotions from the earliest phases of development, for which there are no words or memories.[3] The repetitious, self-defeating aspects of addiction are related to the tongue-in-cheek "definition of insanity" given by addicted people: "it is doing the same thing over and over again and expecting a different outcome." In this chapter we will discuss some of the less obvious reasons for the painful, repetitious madness of addictive behavior.

THE ADDICTIVE PROCESS—PHYSICAL AND PSYCHOLOGICAL DEPENDENCE

As we have stressed throughout this book, there is a physiology and a psychology involved in the process of becoming addicted to substances. In chapter 12 we cover in more detail how addictive substances act in the brain to explain the chemistry of addiction. Before discussing the complexities of how addicted individuals alternate patterns of relieving and experiencing psychological pain, we touch here briefly on the physiology of addiction.

As an individual uses more and more of an addictive drug, two important developments in brain chemistry occur which make it more likely that the use will continue and increase. The first is the problem of *physical tolerance*, which refers to the fact that with regular use of an addictive drug more and more is required to produce the same effect. The second development is that once physical tolerance has developed, *physical dependence* develops, wherein if the person abruptly stops use of the drug, he or she experiences painful symptoms of withdrawal characteristic for that drug. With opiates, for example, there is agitation, irritability, marked sweating and chills, gooseflesh, and an increase in pulse and blood pressure; with alcohol (and other depressants) withdrawal is marked by tremors, sweating, nervousness, seizures, and in extreme cases, delirium; and with stimulants withdrawal produces marked lethargy and depression, insomnia, and social isolation.

The physiological mechanisms of addiction were worked out in the mid-twentieth century in the federal prison/hospital system in Lexington, Kentucky, where pioneering investigators studied addicted individuals incarcerated or confined for substance use disorders. At that time drugs such as cocaine, crystal methamphetamine, and marijuana were not so widely used. Subsequently, these drugs, especially cocaine and crystal methamphetamine, have become all too prevalent and devastatingly consuming and destructive for many people. If there is any good news in this development, it is that we have been better able to both study how these addictive drugs affect the physiology and psychology of individuals and treat drug-dependent individuals in their own communities, rather than in remote treatment centers. Partly as a result of these developments and partly as a result of technological breakthroughs in medicine in general, and in the neurosciences in particular, we have learned much more about the nature of addictive processes. These insights include (1) the notion of protracted withdrawal, referring to subtle, drawn-out physical and psychological distress which can lead to relapse, (2) the sites where the brain is most sensitive and reactive to addictive drugs, and (3) the identification of endogenous (internal) brain chemicals referred to as "neurotransmitters" and "neuroreceptors" corresponding to the exogenous (external) drugs to which individuals become addicted. We discuss these developments and their implications for treatment more extensively in chapter 12.

In this book and in this chapter we underscore mechanisms of psychological dependence which in our experience are at least as compelling, and in many instances more compelling, than problems and mechanisms of physical dependence. In particular we will focus less on the use of addictive drugs to relieve unbearable psychological feelings and pain, a main motive for self-medication, and more on the vague, nameless, and confusing feelings that addiction-prone individuals experience. These better explain the self-defeating and painfully repetitious aspects of addictive behavior.

THE CASE OF SUFFERING SUZIE

Suzie is a proud, divorced forty-two-year-old mother of a teenage son and daughter. She had been struggling for a long time to gain control of her excessive use of alcohol. On the occasion of her son's graduation from high school, she had a mild relapse to alcohol after several months of abstinence. She explained that she thought the relapse was in response to tension and anxiety related to anticipating the arrival of her parents for the graduation, which in part was probably true. On further reflection, however, she recognized that she had, without realizing it, caused herself more pain than relief with the alcohol. She further reflected how her mother "had a long suffering life" as the daughter of two alcoholic parents, adding how much that history has shaped her and her mother's personalities. As Suzie grew up, confusing and troubling matters in her family life had been lived out in problematic and distressful ways but were not expressed in words or talked out. She gave as an example: the fact that nobody in her extended family had known of her twenty years of marital difficulties until the day she left her husband.

She explained how she had thought, anticipating the tension of the family gathering, that "I had it all solved with a few drinks the night before without any major consequences." At first she believed she was not hung over. Quickly she retracted her denial and conceded that she was "upset, shaky, and nauseous" on the morning of graduation. She thought out loud how much her drinking was about "managing suffering." She said the alcoholic part was that she was brought up not only to suffer but to "endure it," adding that it was "what good little girls do," as her mother had learned and taught to Suzie. She said, "That's why when I have a hangover I have trouble being in touch with and acknowledging it, but I have to endure it." She and her therapist agreed that she used alcohol to both relieve and endure her emotional distress, much like she learned as a child.

FEELINGS, REPETITION, AND DRUG DEPENDENCE

The main theme of this book thus far has been how addicted individuals rely on addictive substances to relieve psychological suffering and to regulate their emotions, self-esteem, relationships, and behavior. The most apparent aspects of addiction reside in this need. As much as addiction-prone people discover that in the short term their pain is relieved and they feel better regulated, the price they pay is evident. What becomes just as apparent are the horrible pain and dysregulation they experience in both the short (e.g., hangovers) and long term as a result of their addictive involvements. The following is a partial list of such consequences:

- Emaciation
- Skin infections, ulcers, and scars
- Unkempt and run-down appearance
- Restlessness and anxiousness
- Irritability and agitation
- Downcast and depressed mood
- Distrusting and/or paranoid thinking
- Visual hallucinations
- Hallucinations of bugs under the skin

Some of these reactions can be acute effects of the drug, some the result of chronic use, and some the a result of withdrawal. Each class of
drugs produce any number of these effects, depending upon the drug and
whether it involves a toxic or withdrawal reaction, which we touch upon
elsewhere in this book. Addicted individuals know after a while that these
painful consequences are inescapable, yet they persist with the addiction.
So how can this aspect of addiction be explained from a psychological or
psychodynamic perspective? And does it contradict the SMH?

An early psychodynamic student of addictions, Sandor Rado, suggested that for addicted individuals the "pleasure" was worth the pain.[4]
What he actually meant by pleasure was relief of the psychological pain
and discomfort (what he referred to as "a tense depression") with which
substance abusers suffer. Quite likely this is so. Also, it might be argued
that the physical dependence and distress of withdrawal could be enough
to drive the addiction despite the painful consequences. Our clinical experience has instructed us that often the reason for reverting to drugs,
even after long periods of abstinence, is not necessarily psychological pain
(a motive we have emphasized throughout this book), because it frequently occurs in periods of relative calm and the absence of major distress. Patients describe the impulse to use when they are feeling okay,
good, or bored, knowing that using drugs will ultimately make them feel
worse.

*John, a media celebrity, had established considerable control over heroin use on
his way to abstinence and was no longer physically dependent on the drug. He
had established a stable and caring relationship with a girlfriend, was experiencing a period of calm and satisfaction about his career, and was enjoying a
more harmonious relationship with his parents, which had been elusive for him.
He came to a therapy session with a cast on his arm. He explained that he had
sustained a fracture playing touch football with his friends. Although he was not
in discomfort from the broken arm, or in drug withdrawal, he mentioned that
he had thought of resuming the heroin. Curiously, he emphasized that he did not
want to obliterate intense angry emotions with the heroin, his usual stated motive, but more that he wanted to change how he felt. He said, "You know, doc, I
might get high or I might not, but I know that in the morning I will feel shitty,
but at least I will know what I feel and why I feel it." This was a most reveal-
ing comment, in that most of the time he had trouble identifying and putting
his feelings into words.*

*A therapy group in which John participated shed further light on his mo-
tivation and the other group members' reasons for their on-again, off-again*

relationship with addictive drugs. The group members were describing how their drug of choice relieved a wide range of distressful feeling and states. They were also acknowledging that there was at least as much if not more distress and misery from the complications of their drug use. John particularly stressed this point. Mark, a dentist, blurted out, "We are just as much drawn to the misery the drugs cause us as we are to the relief." He went on to explain, "At least it was a misery I produced and I controlled, but the misery that caused my drug use I could not control." Another patient in the group who was familiar with our writings on the SMH said, "Doc, I know you think we are into relief when we use, but it is 10 percent relief and 90 percent misery."

In our experience such statements from patients in treatment are not unusual, especially in psychotherapy, where we place an emphasis on helping patients to develop a capacity to bear and put into words their feelings and the problems they experience with them. Observing the misery and countless painful mishaps resulting from addictions and listening to the statements coming from patients has forced us to consider the complexities of the pain-relieving and pain-perpetuating aspects of addictive drug use. It suggests that we need to consider that the perpetuation of pain has special motives and can be understood in the context of exploring how troubles with emotions, self-love, and relationships (i.e., the problems with self-regulation we have previously stressed) cause individuals to try and control and change their misery by repeating it. Or, to use the words of addicted individuals, the "insanity has its own reasons." As much as we have emphasized the need to relieve distress through the use of addictive drugs, a motive which is probably at least as important is the negative, painful consequences of addiction, an invariable aspect of the compulsive aspects of addictions. We believe that part of this seeming contradiction in motives is rooted in the ways addiction-vulnerable individuals are different in how they experience, process, and express their emotions, and the way that the painful, repetitious aspects of their addictions help them cope with their lives.* By this we mean substances help individuals deal with intolerable emotional pain as well as pain that is nameless, confusing, and without words. In the next section

---

*As we have previously indicated, many individuals' main motive for self-medicating is that their emotions are extremely intense and unbearable, and/or their incapacity to tolerate painful feelings is a function of underdeveloped defenses. Actually there is a continuum between addicted individuals experiencing emotions as intense and unbearable and emotions being absent or cut-off. Perhaps it is those patients whose feelings are remote, cut-off, vague, and confusing who are more susceptible to perpetuating their pain through their addictive behaviors.

we describe how feeling life is more complex than is apparent and how such complexity contributes to the perpetuation of the repetitious, self-destructive, and painful aspects of addictive behavior.

DISTORTIONS IN FEELING LIFE

The study of the psychology of addiction over the past five decades has revealed some of the unusual and extreme ways addiction-prone people experience and manage their feelings. Parallel studies with other special groups, such as patients with behavioral, personality, and psychosomatic disorders, reveal that they similarly suffer because they experience their emotions in bewildering ways. Terms such as *alexithymia, dysphoria, disaffected, affect deficits, hypophoria,* and *non-feeling responses* are examples of terms that clinical and scientific investigators have adopted to capture some of the different and peculiar ways certain individuals experience and express feelings, especially addictively and behaviorally disordered individuals. For example, a colleague described a patient who received a telegram informing him that his mother had died as saying, "Oh, what a shock that will be in the morning."[5] Such terms and reactions typify how particular individuals, especially substance-dependent ones, may not only be unable to tolerate painful feelings, but also might experience them as absent, confusing, and distorted. This accounts for how experiences that would ordinarily produce extreme emotions can produce no apparent emotions, how such experiences can cause precipitous action, how there can be rapid swings from no reaction to violent eruptions, and how there can be peculiar delays in reaction, as we witnessed in the case of the man who received notice of his mother's death. These descriptions share an appreciation that individuals with certain conditions, especially those with addictive disorders, suffer not only because they are prone to experience feelings as unbearably intense and overwhelming, but also because they do not feel an adequate amount, feel nothing at all, or have feelings that are vague and puzzling.

As we have indicated, people with addiction disorders reveal a wide range of emotional reactions. We have again and again been impressed with how addiction-prone individuals as a group are different in the ways they experience the inner terrain of emotions. By way of accounting for the intensity and peculiarity of their pain and distress, clinicians, including ourselves, have laid emphasis on traumatic and/or deprived growing up environments to account for adult symptoms and conditions such as those associated with the addictions. In our opinion such accounts have not adequately focused on how traumatic abuse or neglect in childhood can warp or alter the experience and expression of feeling in adulthood. Although substance-abusing individuals are often characterized as facile and seductive ("the con"), just as often they are not verbal or engaging, but are constricted and do not connect readily with others, especially emotionally. More often than not, in our experience, patients with substance use disorders consistently reveal some degree of limitation and/or peculiarity in the way they experience, process, and put across their feelings. As we have described, where an experience might evoke strong emotion, such patients appear devoid of feelings; in other cases a stressful situation might suddenly result in a violent outburst. In still other cases a person might focus on the minute details and circumstances of a traumatic or threatening event rather than convey evidence of distress, fear, or hurt.

Dr. Henry Krystal, to whom we have referred previously, is an expert on psychological trauma. He has proposed that feelings develop in certain ways, namely that at the outset of psychological development, feelings are experienced bodily only, are undifferentiated (i.e., feelings such as anxiety and depression are indistinguishable from one another), and are without words.[6] As the child grows and develops into adulthood, feelings are experienced subjectively, emotions become differentiated such that a person can distinguish anxiety from depression, and words are attached to feelings. As Dr. Krystal indicates, either as a function of developmental trauma or traumatic experiences later in life, this process of development can become distorted such that individuals experience or reexperience their emotions through bodily manifestations, and are unable to identify or give words to their feelings (alexithymia). Some of the unusual and bewildering aspects of experiencing and expressing feelings we have just described derive from developmental arrest or regression in feeling life as a result of traumatic abuse or neglect. Working with substance-dependent patients, Dr. Krystal has observed that often they cannot tell or distinguish whether they are sad, tired, hungry, or sick. Little wonder that alcoholics in recovery use and benefit from the acronym HALT, referring to hungry, angry, lonely, and tired, to help them monitor their feelings and how those feelings might affect them. Another psychoanalyst, Joyce McDougal, has described such patients as "dis-affected" in reference to their seeming lack of feelings around emotionally charged events and their tendency to resort to addictive and impulsive behaviors.[7] And Wurmser has referred to the problem of "hypo-symbolization" among addicted individuals wherein they experience difficulties in describing their emotions and fantasies.[8]

As is evident, scholars and clinicians since the last half of the twentieth century, studying special populations such as addicted individuals, have made important contributions to understanding some of the complexities of emotions and how they get linked to behavior. These developments have also been assisted by the work of specialists in childhood development who link the confusing and action-oriented responses of adults to observations from infant research to explain how and why feeling responses can be so baffling. One scholar has eloquently expressed how, as a consequence, "some of life's most meaningful experiences [are] not encoded in words," but extend into adulthood "as perceptual-action-affect" responses.[9] This scholar was observing that early life experiences, dating back to infancy, have a profound effect on our lives as adults. In the absence of memories, these experiences become incorporated into our psychological makeup (personality) in the automatic ways we perceive, act, and behave. Such studies have led to a better understanding of the psychology of repetition, the subject of the next section, a maddening and invariable aspect of addictive behavior.

THE PSYCHOLOGY OF REPETITION

Psychoanalysts have pondered, as have Dostoyevsky and other writers, on the human penchant to pursue and endure suffering. In 1920 Freud introduced the concept of "death instincts" related to aggressive drives to explain human destructiveness.[10] In this same paper he introduced the term "repetition compulsion" to explain how and why we repeat certain behaviors, despite the pain involved. He pointed out how children in their play convert "passive unpleasure" into active mastery. Although he placed much emphasis on human aggression and the instinct for self-destructiveness, one of his most important insights in this respect was on how human repetition has in it an element of helping to cope with and master unpleasant emotions. That is, he deemed it necessary to explain that the pursuit of pleasure was not sufficient to explain the drivenness of human behavior, but that just as much it was rooted in aggressive instincts. In part, such fomulations explains how much of our present-day negative stereotype of the addicted person as a "pleasure-seeker" or "self-destructive character" originates with these early ideas of Freud.

Other psychoanalysts offer a more positive interpretation of repetitious behavior, suggesting that repetition is not in the service of seeking pleasure or self-destruction, but rather to seek contact and comfort, even if it is unsatisfying (i.e., "an obstinate attachment").[11] Or as another student of the problem of masochism observed,

> It is the attempt to bring trauma, that is, pain experienced in the conflict with the external world, into the internal world and thus create the illusion of mastery and control. It is as if one protects oneself from the trauma of overwhelming massive pain by inoculating oneself with repeated small doses.[12]

A patient who had endured repeated childhood physical abuse at the hands of an alcoholic father poignantly brought this point to bear when he reflected upon his painful relapses to alcohol, saying, "I feel tremendous guilt and shame when I relapse, nevertheless I repeat it even though I know how I am going to feel. If I don't feel the guilt, then I feel rage and I want to go after my father . . . [and] the teachers who abused me."

Those who wish to understand and pursue further the psychology of repetition from old and new psychoanalytic perspectives would benefit from the writings of Freud, Fairbairn, Gedo, and Modell, whom we have cited here. In the final section, we consider the purpose and motivations of the painful repetitions in addicted individuals.

ON THE NATURE OF REPETITION IN ADDICTIVE SUFFERING

Psychoanalytic explanations, including our own, have stressed how addicted individuals seek relief from painful feeling with addictive drugs. It might be just as accurate to say that such individuals use substances to change their feelings. In contrast to the adage that addictive substances are "mind [or mood] altering," it is probably more precise to say they are *feeling* altering. Although we have emphasized that the change sought is primarily the release from emotional pain, sooner or later, distress also results. So it appears that if suffering leads to addictive drugs, then suffering results as well. A neuroscientific perspective might simply reduce the latter to an unwanted biological consequence of how addictive drugs affect the brain, both during use and during withdrawal and afterward.

However, studies on the dysfunction and distortions in feelings which we reviewed in the previous section provide a basis to explain why certain individuals, especially substance-dependent ones, characteristically respond to emotional distress with repetitious action and addictive behaviors. Beyond its apparent madness, the repetition has its own reason and serves a purpose. As we have emphasized in this chapter, although addicted people alter their pain, they perpetuate it and often make it worse. They seem at once to be both in control and not in control of the pain. The deficits in feelings and the need to repeat offer an explanation of why addicted persons accept and possibly take advantage of the torment drugs produce while simultaneously depending on the drug's pain-relieving properties. Summarized below is a formulation from a previous publication of how this duality of motives serves addicted individuals.

Once addicts use and become involved with drugs, they discover that the drugs not only can produce relief but also produce and control the vagueness, confusion, and bewilderment associated with their feelings. That is, at the same time that addicts relieve distressing states with drug effects, they also convert the more vague and confusing aspects of their feeling life from a passive experience into an active one. Substance abusers actively replace preexisting passively experienced admixtures of pain, dysphoria, and emptiness with admixtures of analgesia, relief, dysphoria, and distress produced by the drug and its aftereffects. As we previously suggested, language such as "altered states of consciousness" or "mood altering drugs" are commonly used to explain drug urges. In our opinion, the operative word is "alter" and the motive to change "consciousness" or "mood" is misleading. When individuals use drugs, they change qualities and quantities of feelings, and more importantly, they succeed in substituting uncontrolled suffering with controlled suffering, replacing a dysphoria that they do not understand with a drug-induced dysphoria that they do understand.[13]

A central theme of this book has been that addicted people suffer greatly with emotional pain and addictive drugs become a means to relieve their suffering and correct the distress associated with difficulties in regulating their emotions, self-esteem, relationships, and behaviors. In this chapter we have tried to explain how it is that despite the motive to self-medicate psychological pain and distress, individuals who do so nevertheless endure pain as a result of their use. We have proposed that part of the power of addiction and its compulsive nature derives from the need to perpetuate such pain. When this is the case the operative switches from the *relief* of unbearable painful feelings to the *control* of the feelings, particularly when they are nameless, confusing, and vague. Such individuals substitute a kind of pain and distress which they understand and control for a distress they do not understand and do not control. Both the pain-relieving and pain-perpetuating aspects of addiction are attempts to regulate human psychological suffering.

Nicotine, Marijuana, and the SMH

$\mathcal{A}$long with alcohol, nicotine and marijuana are the two most overused and misused addictive substances. Although marijuana abuse and dependence do not generally cause the devastating deleterious consequences that other drugs and addictive behaviors do, the same cannot be said about the tragic and destructive outcomes associated with nicotine dependence. In fact, recent findings have emphasized even marijuana's deleterious effects, including lung damage, acute psychosis, memory problems, and fetal brain damage.[1] Given the pervasiveness of nicotine and marijuana, and the lethal consequences of nicotine, you might wonder why we have not tackled these important addictive substances sooner in this book and whether the SMH applies. There are several reasons for not placing these drugs earlier in this book or including them with the main drugs of dependence which we have reviewed already: (a) Individuals generally do not present themselves to psychiatrists for nicotine or marijuana dependence; (b) to a considerable degree there seems to be less specificity or preference for these two drugs compared to other addictive drugs; (c) in the case of marijuana, there seems to be less physical tolerance and dependence that develops; and finally, (d) given that people are less apt to seek out psychiatrists for dependence on these two drugs, we have had less opportunity to evaluate and explore with patients what their motivations have been for using and becoming psychologically dependent on nicotine and marijuana.

In this chapter we will briefly review the clinical and empirical evidence which indicates that there is a considerable degree of self-medication involved when individuals begin to overuse and become dependent on nicotine and marijuana, and whether addiction to these drugs is similar to addiction to other substances and behaviors.

NICOTINE DEPENDENCE

The day we set out to write this chapter, an article on nicotine addiction in the *Boston Globe* began with the statement, "Smoking is linked to one in five U.S. deaths a year," a startling statistic which should prompt believers to consider the immediate cessation of smoking. Smoking significantly increases the chances of developing cancer, heart disease, and many other serious medical conditions. The costs of medical care for these complications are placed at $75.5 billion each year. Even though there has been a major drop in the smoking rate over the past forty years (the rate in 1965 was about 42 percent), there has not been much change since 1990, when the rate was estimated to be about 24 percent. So once again we consider an addictive substance, nicotine, whose use and overuse defies reason and appears to consume those who cannot relinquish the hold of this addiction. There is considerable evidence that biological factors and distress associated with psychological and psychiatric issues make susceptibility to nicotine likely. As a function of advances in neurosciences, there is evidence that the ways of delivering the nicotine (i.e., mainly inhaling/smoking) and the transmitter/receptor systems involved in the brain interact with psychological and psychiatric vulnerabilities to greatly heighten the tendency to become addicted to this drug.

Although we have always considered nicotine a stimulant, we agree with Dr. John Hughes, one of the foremost authorities on nicotine dependence, that it is less specific than most addictive substances in its effects. For this reason Dr. Hughes has referred to nicotine as a renaissance drug.[2] He persuasively brings this point home with the following observation about the effects of nicotine:

- Improves concentration
- Relieves anxiety and depression
- Relieves anger
- Decreases appetite

He then observes that the problems of sixteen-year-olds are:

- Concentrating on school work
- Controlling moods
- Aggression (especially boys)
- Weight gain (especially girls)

This is not unlike the patient who, when asked what cigarettes did for him, replied, "When I need a pickup, it picks me up and when I need something to bring me down, it brings me down." Here again is a place where findings from neuroscience converge with clinical findings and experiences. Namely nicotine acts on nicotinic acetylcholine receptors in the brain in the mesocorticolimbic dopaminergic system which projects into the nucleus acumbens and the prefrontal cortex. In less technical terms, as we will see in chapter 12, these parts of the brain are important in processing reward, pleasure, and emotions and involve areas that literally "light up" when brain imaging techniques are used to study the effects of drugs in the brain. Importantly, there are subtypes of the nicotinic receptors with different functions, distributions, and sensitivity to nicotine, likely accounting for the diverse effects of nicotine observed clinically.[3]

That Dr. Hughes links the appeal to teenage years is of great significance in that the special aspects of nicotine consumption (mainly smoking) and the frequency and dose of delivery make it highly addictive to a most susceptible group, namely our youth. When inhaled, nicotine is directly transported to the brain in a concentrated dose, bypassing peripheral circulation. Considering the consumption of a pack or more, and assuming five to ten puffs per cigarette, hundreds of doses go to the brain per day. Continuing into adulthood, we know of no other drug addiction that involves such frequency and regularity of use throughout a person's life. Beyond these physiological and biological factors that make nicotine so addictive, add the fact that nicotine relieves a wide range of distressful feelings, from the mild to moderate psychological pain of everyday life to the more intense suffering associated with major mental illness such as schizophrenia and depression, there is little wonder that nicotine addiction can be so persistent and ultimately deadly.

Although many individuals are saved from becoming addicted to nicotine because they do not tolerate its negative side effects when they first smoke it (e.g., dizziness, jitteriness, throat and lung irritation), unfortunately too many individuals tolerate these side effects or do not experience them sufficiently to be deterred. Like in the case of other addictive drugs, there is a basis to conclude that those who go on to smoke regularly do so because, beyond the physiologic aspects of addiction, nicotine relieves them of emotional distress and the suffering associated with various psychiatric conditions.

It has been long observed that patients suffering with schizophrenia smoke heavily. In contrast to the current rates of approximately 24 percent of the general population smoking, the estimated rates of smoking among individuals with schizophrenia range as high as 75 to 90 percent. These individuals also exhibit great difficulty in stopping.[4] Nicotine alleviates side effects of medications used to treat schizophrenia; it also relieves the negative symptoms of schizophrenia such as boredom, anhedonia, blunted emotions, and attentional problems. As we discussed in chapter 7, these symptoms produce extraordinary distress for which patients often cannot find words, but to a small degree they do find relief from them with smoking.

Important studies over the past two decades have shown a significant association between major depression, depressive symptomotology, and nicotine dependence. For example, a twenty-one-year study that followed over 1,200 children from birth found that individuals with depression in adolescence were at significantly greater risk of later developing nicotine dependence.[5] Also, based on a large national database, investigators found smoking rates increased and quit rates decreased as depressive symptoms increased, and significantly, with the benefit of nine-year follow-up, they observed that nondepressed smokers had a quit rate twice that of the depressed smokers (17.7 percent vs. 9.9 percent, respectively).[6] In another study researchers found a strong association between major depression and both cigarette smoking and a lower rate of success in quitting. Strikingly, the lead author in this study described observing, clinically, the gradual development of "serious depression" after stopping smoking in a number of cases and the disappearance of depression within hours after resuming smoking.[7] Dr. Richard Glass, the associate editor of the *Journal of the American Medical Association*, in a commentary article accompanying the two articles referenced here, concluded that the SMH fits these studies and that smokers were using nicotine to relieve the distress of major depression and less severe depressive symptoms.[8]

Dr. Judith Brooks and her associates have tracked several trajectories for smokers and nonsmokers and demonstrated that heavy smokers were often individuals who started smoking in adolescence, exhibited more unconventional behavior, and experienced more psychological distress.[9] An extensive review of more studies would go beyond the scope of this chapter, but we would cite the work of one more investigator whose work supports the conclusion that heavy smoking and nicotine dependence are associated with psychological distress. Dr. Naomi Breslau, using scales to measure subjective distress, not necessarily psychiatric disorders, found that neuroticism, negative affect, hopelessness, and general emotional distress were associated with nicotine dependence.[10]

MARIJUANA ABUSE

In contrast to nicotine, the negative consequence of regular or heavy use of and dependence on marijuana continues to be controversial and debated, considered minimal by some experts and serious by others.[11] Aside from medical complications, especially lung problems, experts in the serious camp have considered incentive and initiative problems (amotivational syndrome) as well as more familiar psychiatric complications, including the development of panic disorder, depression, and psychosis.

As noted above, it is becoming increasingly clear that marijuana is not as harmless as has been touted. Our society seems to have a great ambivalence about this substance, which has probably retarded our investigation and understanding of it. The generation for whom marijuana came into vogue has come into its own and is apparently unscathed. This has left our society with the skewed notion that this is a relatively benign substance. The ambivalence is illustrated by a recent interaction that one of us (MJA) experienced when asked to consult for a treatment facility. While the facility had clear guidelines about treatment tracks for people with persistent, ongoing use of substances such as heroin, cocaine, and alcohol, it was bewildered about what to do about ongoing marijuana use. The covert attitude seemed to be "after all, its marijuana, and everybody uses marijuana, right?" We now understand that marijuana, which is more potent today than it ever has been, can do bad stuff to you.

But what does marijuana do for you? It turns out that there is an endogenous cannabinoid system with at least two kinds of brain receptors. Given what our patients tell us about the mellowing quality of marijuana, it should come as no surprise that the cannabinoid system seems to modulate anxiety and fear. [12] Also, a recent study on rats suggests that stress-related pain is relieved by the naturally occurring cannabinoids. [13]

Intriguingly, investigators found that in non-identical twins, if one twin reported major depression or suicidal ideation before age seventeen, that twin was significantly more likely to develop marijuana dependence than the twin who did not report such early depression or suicidal ideation.[14] For identical twins, however, there was no difference in development of marijuana dependence between the twin with depression/suicidal ideation and the one without.

Clearly, the marijuana story is a complex one. Even before researchers started to teach us about marijuana, our patients had introduced us to this complexity. While marijuana is a magical drug for some people, it is a distressful substance to be avoided for others.

In our opinion there is rich and ample clinical and empirical data to suggest that nicotine and marijuana dependence are associated with a range of painful and distressing feeling states. Some are associated with psychiatric disorders, but just as importantly, a variety of negative emotions, which are discomforting and painful in their own right, are not. We believe there is a basis to conclude that people are wittingly and unwittingly self-medicating psychiatric conditions and other forms of subjective distress with nicotine and marijuana.

Behavioral Addictions: Does the SMH Apply?

When joy is felt by a suffering child, he/she will do anything to have that feeling again, even if it is behavior that is beyond comprehension. When behavior works to relieve intense suffering, no matter how bizarre it is, it will be repeated, often to an obsessive degree. So often behavioral disorders that confound explanation can be understood by knowing the experiences of the child or person. Some will never be able to fully explain what they experience. Those who do help us to better explain the others and it is through our listening and interest that compassion grows.

Corinne F. Gerwe[1]

𝒟r. Gerwe appreciates as well as anyone the suffering entailed in addictive behavior, and she has employed this understanding in her orchestration method to empathically treat individuals who endure addictive disorders.[2] Like us, she has worked to fathom the seemingly incomprehensible progressive, consuming, and painful repetitious behaviors, as cause and consequence, associated with addictive disorders. In this chapter we will single out two behavioral addictions, namely pathological sexual behavior and gambling. The interested reader and student is referred to a recent textbook in which related compulsive and addictive behaviors such as eating disorders, shopping, and computer addiction are extensively reviewed; for the most part these behaviors seem to share many of the characteristics of addiction to substances.[3] The clinical features, with empirical data to support the concept, suggest that such behavioral disorders have much in common with chemical addictions. In our opinion the evidence provides a basis to conclude that these addictive behaviors, much like substances of addiction, serve the need to relieve or change distress associated with enduring painful feelings and problems with self-esteem and interpersonal relationships. We believe there is reason to presume that the SMH paradigm applies to behavioral addictions.

Much like addiction to substances, one of the most prominent aspects of behavioral addictions is their persistence and recurrence despite the deleterious, damaging consequences. For example, are the desperation, shame, and humiliation of the compulsive gambler who has remortgaged his home for the third time and stolen petty cash from his son's Little League fund that different from those of the class valedictorian who has succumbed to an addiction to Oxycontin and is arrested robbing the local pharmacy? Or consider the lot of the school superintendent who is caught in a sting operation involving child pornography on the Internet. In this chapter we examine how behavioral addictions are similar in many respects to substance addictions, including the way addictive behaviors serve a function in alleviating psychological pain and suffering. Behavioral addictions are a form of self-medication for distressful states.

SEXUAL ADDICTION

The Case of Bennett

Bennett was an accomplished academic neurologist, well respected by both colleagues and students. He should have felt better about himself and his accomplishments, but he did not. His poor self-esteem derived from his history of feeling undervalidated by his mother, for whom success and performance were what mattered most. For example, she detracted from the joy of graduating second in his high school class by mentioning that he could have been number one. As an adult his problems with his self-image were further compounded by his marriage to a woman in the medical center whose accomplishments overshadowed his own. It was a relationship in which he also often felt subservient and deferential, given the many pressures in her work.

In the course of using the Internet to do research, he discovered some dating websites. Impulsively, during a period of feeling particularly lonely and underappreciated in his marriage, he contacted a woman through a website. He soon learned how easy it was to make such connections, and how casual sex was a foregone conclusion in these liaisons. More captivating for him was how reassured and excited he was by the admiration and validation that followed from the now more frequent meetings with these women. Although he had had a few extramarital relationships early in his marriage, none made him feel the same degree of exhilaration he experienced with these liaisons. He insisted that although the sex was satisfying, it was being admired for his personal qualities that most appealed to him. This fix for his self-esteem was so powerful that he found himself spending more and more time on the Internet at home and at work. Predictably, he revealed his relationships through inadvertent interceptions of e-mails by his wife and a supervisor at work. The humiliation and shame he experienced was considerable, as was the fear of putting both his marriage and career in jeopardy. The marital and work concerns caused him to seek out psychotherapy with an addiction specialist because he and his wife decided that he had acted much like an addicted person in his secretive and risky behavior. It was also a condition that his wife set for reversing the separation the crisis precipitated.

As we indicated at the beginning of this book, we consider addictions as self-regulation disorders in which the addictive behavior is an attempt to correct or to deal with difficulties in regulating emotions, self-esteem, relationships, and self-care. Although Bennett was in touch with his emotions and capable of good relationships with his peers and friends, he struggled with this vexing, hidden issue of shaky self-esteem throughout his life. His sexual connections seemed to offer a temporary correction, more than anything else, for how empty, lonely, and unlovable he felt.

We develop a sense of well-being and self-respect by establishing a cohesive sense of ourselves in which we feel comfortable inside our skin, like ourselves, and feel that others respect and love us. For individuals such as Bennett this positive sense about self can be tragically elusive and lead to a range of "errant behaviors,"[4] including addictive ones, in an attempt to correct a fundamental personality flaw. For a more extensive review of the range of addictive vulnerabilities, including behavioral ones, the interested reader would benefit from recent psychoanalytic publications in which psychological deficits and conflicts involving the intolerance of painful feelings, faulty self-esteem development, and relational difficulties involved in addictive behaviors are covered in more detail.[5]

The Case of Tom

Tom is a twenty-five-year-old gay man who from a young age seemed to be on a fast track to becoming a prominent man of the arts, most likely as a museum curator or an art critic. His passion for the arts seemed to be exceeded only by his fascination with matters sexual. His career was almost entirely derailed, however, by a newfound obsession with cocaine while he was a student in a prestigious fine arts preparatory school. Although he managed to complete preparatory school with honors, by the end of his first year in an equally prestigious fine arts college, his addictive descent into cocaine use, and the resulting agitation and physical deterioration, forced a withdrawal from his studies. With an extended stay in rehabilitation and involvement in twelve-step programs, he gradually righted himself sufficiently to allow some reunion with his family (he reluctantly moved home, where he had to contend with a doting, hypercontrolling mother and a perfectionistic father) and to gain employment as a manager of a twenty-four-hour convenience store, a station in life which he considered far removed from his aspirations to be independent, pursuing his studies and working in the art world. He sought out psychotherapy to understand and work out his addiction to cocaine and learn how to avoid the traps that had derailed his education and ambitions.

When he arrived for his therapy he presented as a handsome, well-built, bright, articulate man who spoke thoughtfully and remorsefully about his succumbing to cocaine. He was taking courses part-time to prepare for reentrance, if possible, to his college. When talking about his approach to his studies, or for that matter, his approach to his job as a store manager, he was intent on presenting a most earnest and perfectionist image. With his gifts as a student and his intensity as a person, he excelled in whatever he did with only modest effort, whether it was writing a scholarly paper for class or managing the store efficiently. As he became less defensive about his image—and in the context of frustration with his therapist about his bill—he admitted having doubts about the usefulness of the therapy. At the same time he acknowledged that he was not being entirely truthful about himself and his activities. He confessed that he was addicted to the Internet, that his obsession with sex was causing him to spend inordinate time on pornographic websites, and that he periodically toyed with pursuing some liaisons through the Internet. Shortly after these disclosures he regained admission to his school, and in therapy began a more fruitful exploration of his addictive behaviors. He was once again excelling superlatively in an extremely competitive academic environment, and was becoming just as earnest in his therapy. He revealed that previously he had often not disclosed in therapy information about his thoughts and behaviors because he feared the therapist would think less of him. He said that shame and pride had guided, if not tormented, him much of his life. It gradually became clear that the effects of cocaine were harnessed in the service of what he believed was his primary addiction, sex. At one point he blurted out, "I can't banish drugged-out sex from my mind." Although he was successfully abstaining from cocaine with the aid of intense immersion in twelve-step meetings, he was not so easily staying away from his sexual addiction. He was aware that the two had become associated and that one addiction could trigger the other, but his sexual addiction, which he was resisting, remained his and his therapist's concern. In one visit, he offered that a friend with similar problems had shared that "staying away from the Internet was harder than not drinking or drugging ever was."

In this context he spoke of how the theme of body beauty and the attention it drew was an extremely important part of the pull of his sexual preoccupations and fantasies. This preoccupation was also reflected in his diligence developing and maintaining his own sculpted body with persistent and regular intense workouts. Not unlike the escalation observed with other addictions, he needed more and more stimulating images and risky websites to meet his needs for excitation (i.e., suggesting the development of tolerance—the need for more to get the same effect); he also conceded how after periods of abstaining from the Internet, any minor slips using the Internet quickly became "unmanageable." He acknowledged how aware he was that such slips and relapses would jeopardize his academic standing. As Tom and his therapist further investigated the dimensions and nature of his sexual compulsions it became clear how the "empowering" nature of intense and exciting gay liaisons, and the cocaine which fueled it, were powerful antidotes to a chronic sense of feeling disempowered by the unbearable influences of his mother. In a session just before a summer break, he speculated that his sexual fantasies and behaviors were a way of avoiding the image and discomfort of his doting, suffocating mother implanted in his mind.

As we highlight in this chapter and elsewhere in this book, addictions take many forms. However, whether it is an addiction to a substance or to a behavior, we keep learning that the compulsions involved in the addictions are rooted in lifelong distress and suffering, both as a cause and consequence. Tom's primary addiction turned out to be a sexual one and cocaine became a means to augment and maintain its frenzied pursuit. But the addiction nearly killed him at the same time it almost destroyed any remaining sense of self-worth and commitment to his ambitions and career. Aware that the intensity and escalation of his sexual desires was consuming, dangerous, and destructive, he persisted for a long time in his sexual addiction despite the deadly consequences, one of the most prominent hallmarks of an addiction. Fortunately, he has been able to reclaim his gifts, intensity, and intelligence in resuming his work and devotion to the arts and is again on track to succeed. He is also aware of the power of his sexual addiction, and that he is one click away on the computer from a devastating relapse.

As became evident in treatment, Tom used sexual liaisons and be-havior to counter a chronic sense of feeling weak and helpless. Dr. Lance Dodes, a modern-day psychoanalyst, has written eloquently and persua-sively on how addictive behavior is rooted in life-long feelings of help-lessness such as Tom experienced.[6] Dodes proposes that such long-term feeling states engender damage to one's sense of self (he calls it "narcissis-tic injury"), and that addictive behavior actively restores a better sense of oneself by turning around the feelings of helplessness and reestablishing a sense of power and control. He further elaborates that addictive behavior is an expression of narcissistic rage, and that it is this combination of help-lessness and rage which fuels addiction's compulsion. Dodes considers ad-dictive behaviors to be types of compulsions, and believes that such an un-derstanding should be at the heart of treating patients in therapy. While Tom was using sexual addiction to attempt to correct a sense of power-lessness, others might use such behavior to correct elusive and/or over-whelming feelings, as we have described with drug use. Other people might use a behavior to repair a daunting sense of gloom and despair, as the next case demonstrates.

GAMBLING ADDICTION

Although gambling disorders are more commonly referred to as problem gambling or pathological gambling, individuals who experience them manifest the same continuum of patterns seen with addictive substances, including "social or recreational" gambling, "at-risk" gambling, and "com-pulsive" (or addictive) gambling. Addictive gamblers share with people addicted to alcohol and drugs such symptoms as an excessive preoccupa-tion with planning and pursuing activities to insure the behavior; persist-ence in the behavior despite deleterious and destructive consequences; and feelings of distress and withdrawal when they cannot pursue the behavior. From the perspective of this book, addictive gambling also shares with other addictions the dual aspect of the behavior's both relieving suffering and perpetuating it, as the following vignette reveals.

The Case of David

David is a certified public accountant (CPA) who endured much hardship and trauma in his childhood and adolescence. His father was a harsh, moody, self-

centered man who was verbally abusive to David, an only child, and David's mother. He drank and smoked heavily and, when not around to abuse them, was totally immersed in his metropolitan real estate business. He was also a notorious womanizer, which he did not work hard at disguising, thus burdening David and his mother with added cruelty. At age thirteen, David's woe and distress was greatly heightened when his father was found dead in a rented room, presumably from suicide, but with lingering suspicions of foul play. David still remembers vividly the climate of gloom, shock, bewilderment, and shame he felt at the time of his father's death. He recalls sitting outside his high school all alone, school in session, wondering why he could not enjoy the normal life and happiness he imagined the students in the building enjoyed.

Shortly after his father's death a friend introduced him to offtrack betting, which he discovered was a grand distraction from his misery. Although he and the friend were underage, they were able to gamble through an older man in the neighborhood who was willing to place their bets. Because he was bright and facile with mathematics he quickly began mastering the mysteries of the racing sheets, odds making, and trying to pick winners. Soon he was devoting inordinate amounts of time and money to gambling, losing more than a generous allowance and part-time salary could allow. When he became old enough he switched from betting on thoroughbred horses to gambling in a casino in a neighboring state. Again he escalated his betting, sustaining heavy losses and mounting debt from credit cards and loan sharks. His marriage failed, and the shame, remorse, and sense of humiliation resulting from his gambling were palpable and undisguisable. Despite his gambling addiction, he managed to complete his education at a prominent university, majoring in business and accounting. He described periods of abstinence from gambling when he worked mercilessly to reduce his debt alternating with periods of painful relapse. Seeking out consultation with an addiction specialist, he described how his gambling cycles repeated the feelings of loss, loneliness, and gloomy mood he experienced as a teen in the aftermath of his father's suicide. He said, "I feel better for a while, anticipating going to the casino, figuring the odds at the tables, placing my bets, some excitement when I win—but then I lose. I feel horrible, guilty that I've lost control again . . . like I'll never recover from my (mounting) debt. . . . I panic." Spontaneously, he added, "It's like I retraumatize myself . . . I feel like I felt as a teenager, all alone in my room, everything so dark and gloomy, so hopeless."

David's difficulties with compulsive gambling have many features in common with both Tom's and Bennett's addiction to compulsive sexual activities, and with so many of the individuals with drug addictions that we have described in this book. Dr. Howard Shaffer and his collaborators at Harvard Medical School have described a syndrome model of addictive behavior, which develops this theme about the commonalities among the addictive disorders.[7] They point out that there are neurobiological risk factors, common across the full spectrum of addictions, that predispose people to the development of addictions. These combine with psychological and social risk factors, also common among people with different addictive manifestations, such that when a vulnerable person encounters an object of addiction, that person is at significant risk of becoming addicted to the object, whether it is heroin, gambling, or sex. Shaffer's syndrome model of addiction is entirely consistent with the SMH. We have illustrated that there are common factors residing in individuals having to do with their biology, psychology, and surrounding environment that make addictive behavior highly likely when those individuals encounter activities or substances that, through their effects on the individual's brain and emotions, make themselves an object of misuse. These behaviors and substances help individuals to relieve or change the psychological suffering and pain caused by the biological, social, spiritual, and psychological factors that have combined to result in vulnerable people, much like addictive drugs do. In this book, we have emphasized the psychological factors, but not at the expense of the spiritual, social, or biological. Individuals discover what substance or behavior works best to relieve their suffering, becoming captive to that object both psychologically and physically as they discover that they can no longer function without it.

In common with other people we have described, David experienced major parental neglect, abuse, and abandonment. Another common and prominent feature of his addiction was how his pattern of gambling alternately relieved and perpetuated his suffering. Just as Suzie, John, and Mark described their experiences with addictive drugs in chapter 9, David speculated that that there was a troubled motive in the way he perpetuated and repeated his pain with the compulsive gambling.

Addictions to behaviors such as sex, gambling, shopping, and eating are different expressions of a common need to relieve and control human psychological suffering. As Shaffer suggests, like Sandor Rado before him,[8] it is not the drug (or the behavior) alone that determines susceptibility to addiction, but the vulnerable person and the impulse and need to use it. This meeting of vulnerable person and behavior or substance is powerfully intense and overrides all other considerations in a person's life. Should we be surprised that in the lives of Tom, Bennett, and David feelings of de-

spair, loneliness, helplessness, and pain loomed so large, or that they attempted to relieve their suffering through addictive behaviors which simultaneously heightened their distress? We think not. This is so because
they had the same experience as individuals dependent on addictive drugs
who in the short-term find that their addiction makes them able to cope
and their lives more endurable by relieving and controlling their pain, even
if it sometimes makes that pain worse.

· 12 ·

The Neurobiology of Addiction
and the SMH

$\mathcal{O}$ver the last two decades we have made tremendous strides in understanding how the brain works. Similarly, we have made significant
progress in understanding human genetics. As we have begun to learn
about the neurobiology and genetics of addictions, clinicians are both better able to understand what they have observed for generations and better
able to tailor care for people. In this chapter, we will review the actions of
substances of abuse in the brain as well as how genetic variations might
explain some of the vulnerability to addiction. We will also explain how
medication development has evolved from our current understanding of
addiction neurobiology. And we will conclude by attempting to integrate
our understanding of neurobiology with our psychosocial approach to addictions.

HOW SUBSTANCES OF ABUSE WORK IN THE BRAIN

Substances of abuse produce their effects by taking advantage of neurochemical transmitters and receptor sites in the brain. So, the first point to
remember is that addictive substances typically mimic endogenous brain
substances and interact in the brain at receptor sites for these endogenous
substances. Panksepp and colleagues submit that substances of abuse com-
mandeer normal functions of brain receptor systems.[1]

For example, there are endogenous opioid transmitters and opioid receptors. The opioid pain relievers such as morphine and illicit opioids such
as heroin are structurally similar to the class of endogenous opioids known

as the endorphins. When opioids act at these receptors the resultant clinical picture is someone—distanced from their physical and emotional pain—who is calm, possibly drowsy, and has a decreased respiration rate. As the dose of opioids gets higher and higher, the result can be stupor, coma, respiratory depression, and respiratory arrest.

Similarly there are endogenous cannabinoids, the endocannabinoids, which act at endogenous cannabinoid receptors in the brain. This is also the site of action of ingested cannabinoids, such as marijuana. Alcohol takes advantage of receptors in the brain that release a major inhibitory neurotransmitter, gamma amino butyric acid (GABA), and another set of receptors that result in the blockade of the action of the brain's major excitatory neurotransmitter, glutamate. Thus, when a person ingests alcohol, central nervous system inhibition results. Therefore, we observe a decrease in reaction time, decrease in anxiety, and with enough alcohol, stupor or coma. When alcohol is withdrawn from the brain, we observe the converse, namely glutamate is allowed to act at its receptors, with resultant signs of excitation, such as increased anxiety, insomnia, and restlessness, and, later, seizures.

HOW DOES ACTION AT RECEPTORS DEVELOP INTO ADDICTION?

In chapter 5 we briefly reviewed the contribution of genes to addictive vulnerability. Studies indicate that genetic variations in these endogenous neurotransmitter systems are responsible for overreliance on ingested, exogenous, substances in certain individuals.[2] Thus, differences in genes can account for differences in receptor and neurotransmitter responses from person to person. And these differences can account for differential response to substances. For example, an endogenous opioid system that performs at a low level can be normalized by ingesting a compound such as Oxycontin or heroin. In the end, as the brain becomes increasingly reliant on the ingested opioid, the person cannot function normally without it, and a vicious cycle has begun. As Glass has suggested: "Exogenous drugs overwhelm the normal function, and the beneficial effects sought by the user become outweighed by the adverse effect of drug abuse."[3]

The brain reinforces ingestion of substances in other ways as well. One system implicated in this reinforcement is the so-called brain reward pathway. This pathway, which is activated by life-sustaining activities such as sex and eating, consists of neurons that originate in the ventral tegmental area (VTA) of the brain and terminate in the nucleus accumbens (NAc). When stimulated, these neurons release dopamine. The feeling of pleasure associated with substance ingestion is correlated with this dopamine release. It turns out that addictive substances—and certain excessive activities, such as gambling—all stimulate the release of dopamine in this system and also change the way a person feels.

Amphetamines act on these neurons directly to release dopamine. Cocaine, in a variation on this theme, prevents the removal of dopamine once it has been released into the NAc. Other substances act less directly, but with the same resulting dopamine release. For example, there are opioid receptors on the neurons in the VTA. When endogenous or ingested opioids attach to these receptors, they stimulate the cells to release dopamine in the NAc. Alcohol causes the release of endogenous opioids, thus also stimulating the release of dopamine indirectly.

With ongoing substance use, over time the neurotransmitter/receptor systems change. Neurotransmitter release decreases, as does the number of receptors. So, people need more of the drug to get the same effect. This is what we described previously as tolerance. If a person decreases or abruptly stops substance use, he or she has decreased receptor occupancy and starts to experience signs and symptoms opposite to those experienced when intoxicated. We describe this as withdrawal. Thus a person who is calm, drowsy, and breathing slowly when heroin has been ingested will exhibit agitation, irritability, insomnia, and more rapid breathing when she decreases or totally stops heroin use. Therefore, in addition to action within the reward pathway, the need to correct for tolerance and the avoidance of unpleasant withdrawal become other forces promoting ongoing substance use.

Similarly, Koob and LeMoal have suggested that within the reward pathway, changes occur to make it more difficult to elicit the same amount of dopamine release.[4] That is, with time, dopamine function changes, such that its release and receptor numbers both decrease, and it takes more and more substance to keep up the release of dopamine and avoid the dysphoria seen clinically when the brain reward pathway experiences decreased dopamine release.[5] Meanwhile, while the dopamine system has been activated, the body makes an effort to stay in balance. The counterbalancing is through the so-called stress response system, which includes the amygdala, hypothalamus, pituitary, and—outside the brain—adrenal glands.[6] The response from this system outlasts the activation of the dopamine system, which further contributes to the discomfort of withdrawal.

Other brain areas are also implicated in the tendency for some people to abuse substances. In addition to the NAc, the VTA sends dopaminergic projections to the prefrontal cortex (PFC), the region of the brain responsible for learning and executing new behaviors, and the amygdala, which communicates with memory and emotion circuits.[7] Substances of abuse produce a bigger increase in dopamine transmission than other rewarding substances. Furthermore, the PFC, which is also important for judgment and planning, fails to exercise its usual inhibition in dopamine release in this pathway over time, resulting in over-learning of drug-ingesting behavior.[8] So, we can see how brain dysfunction in these areas could contribute to the self-care deficits we have observed clinically and which we described in chapter 3.

MEDICATION DEVELOPMENT BASED ON NEUROBIOLOGY

Our understanding of the underlying neurobiology that contributes to the genesis and maintenance of addiction has helped to guide the development of medications to aid in the treatment of addictions. Rather than provide an exhaustive overview of medications for addictions, we will provide a few illustrative examples. In chapter 13, we will discuss medication treatment further.

If you understand that addiction to opioids might be driven by a person's attempt to boost an underperforming endogenous opioid system, then you might speculate that a well-designed exogenous opioid booster may be efficacious in treating opioid-dependent people. In fact, decades of experience have borne out the efficacy of methadone in treating opioid dependence. Methadone is a synthetic, long-acting opioid that when gradually dosed occupies and activates the mu-opioid receptors, blocking the highs and lows of quicker- and shorter-acting chemicals like heroin, limiting the development of tolerance, and normalizing a deficient system. Naltrexone, on the other hand, blocks the same opioid receptors, turning off the opioid system and preventing the binding of opioids to the receptors, thus eliminating the rewarding nature of the opioids. Interestingly, alcohol's mechanism of activating the opioid receptors that leads to stimulation of dopamine release in the reward pathway made the blockade of this mechanism a target of medication development. Thus, naltrexone was also studied in alcohol-dependent people and found to be effective in this population as well.

Of note, as we will see in chapter 13, the studies establishing the role of medications in treating addictions have taught us what clinicians observe every day. While medications can facilitate recovery by helping to balance profoundly unbalanced systems, for most patients medications alone are not sufficient treatment for their addictive disorders. Excellent studies on methadone, for example, have demonstrated that patients do the best when a large enough dose of methadone is combined with an assortment of services based on the needs of individual patients. Thus, for people with deficits in work skills, employment counseling might be necessary. For those with troubled family relationships, family therapy might be called for.

INTEGRATING NEUROBIOLOGY, PSYCHOLOGY, SOCIAL CONTEXT, AND SPIRIT

These studies combining medications and psychosocial treatments suggest that neurobiology alone is insufficient in either explaining the experience of addiction or treating it. In fact, the more we learn about how drugs work in the brain, the more we realize how much we do not understand. Even if we did understand the neurobiology completely, it would be naïve to think that this would fully explain and resolve addictive disorders. Similarly, as the studies alluded to above have demonstrated, even medication developed with a correct understanding of addiction neurobiology cannot completely address the litany of difficulties that are part and parcel of a life with addiction. At a very basic level a person has to exercise his or her free will, that most unpredictable of human qualities, to take the medication in the first place.

So, how do we start to integrate what we have observed clinically with what we are learning from neurobiology? The picture is a work in progress, but the corners are filling in. For example, we have described difficulties with regulating emotions, self-esteem, and relationships observed among addicted individuals (see chapter 3). A recent study in rats found that *low* levels of a brain protein called brain-derived neurotropic factor is associated with an *increase* in both anxiety and alcohol consumption.[9] In another intriguing study, people were asked to observe emotional stimuli and label the emotion demonstrated.[10] Brain activity in the limbic system of the brain—the area responsible for experiencing emotional reactivity—was reduced (i.e., emotional distress was diminished) in people allowed to not just observe, but to put a label to emotions. Psychotherapists have taught for over a century that discussing your emotions makes you feel better. The neurobiologists are now helping to understand how brain activity affects this process, *and is affected by it.*

There are other examples of neurobiology's contribution to our understanding of emotional regulation: Evidence is accumulating that points toward decreased dopamine transmission having a role in major depression—a disorder in which emotional dysregulation is taken to an extreme. In fact, one could conceptualize severe major depression as an emotional dysregulation emergency. As we know, amphetamine boosts dopamine transmission in the reward pathway. It turns out that nonaddicted people with severe major depression, under experimental conditions, describe an experience of greater "reward" after ingesting amphetamine than do nondepressed or mildly depressed people.[11] It is not much of a stretch to speculate that in everyday life some depressed people with certain blends of genes, biology, distress, and social circumstances would end up discovering amphetamine, liking it, then liking it too much, with detrimental but understandable results.

In the case of PTSD, investigators seem to be further along.[12] As we mentioned in chapter 8, traumatized children exhibit dysregulation of the stress response system, with subsequent negative affective symptoms. This may explain the increased use of alcohol and drugs in an effort to self-medicate the distressful feelings. As we have described, substance use further dysregulates the stress system. The increased cortisol from this system can contribute to developmental problems in the brain's frontal and prefrontal cortex, with resultant failures in self-regulation and increases in impulsivity.

Perhaps other areas of dysregulation—relationships, for example—have some neurobiological basis? Investigators have speculated that the dopamine reward system may be implicated in social interaction that has gone awry. As it turns out, rats that are exposed to social attachment show an increase in dopamine transmission. Those with pathways that do not allow dopamine transmission exhibit poor social attachment.[13] Similarly, neurobiology is better defining the brain substrates for the self-care deficits observed in addicted people. Neuropsychological testing has revealed widespread deficits in the executive function of brains of addicted people.[14]

BEYOND NEUROBIOLOGICAL AND
PSYCHOLOGICAL REDUCTIONISM

In the end, as illustrated above, the exciting developments in genetics, neurobiology, and pharmacology are providing us with significant tools to address the suffering resulting from addiction. At the same time, however, the addictions field will be shortchanged if we decide that establishing the existence of a neurobiological substrate proves our legitimacy or is the end of a long developmental road. We were amused and troubled recently when people said to us that a recent HBO series on addictions would establish the medical nature of addictive disorders, thus presumably explaining and establishing it as a "brain disease" for the general public. In reality, we need to get beyond an oversimplified, judgmental view of addicted people, and understand their distress. Truly, we are just at the beginning of our understanding of integrated, whole human beings who suffer with addictive disorders.

We can learn from our medical colleagues. When we completed our medical training, most of the excitement was about new developments in biological assessment tools (e.g., CT and MRI scans) and biological therapeutics (e.g., anti-hypertensives and diabetes medications). What has emerged more recently is an appreciation for the psychosocial components of very biological diseases. We have learned that women with breast cancer who have been given excellent surgical and medical treatments live longer if they receive group therapy; we have also learned that depression and anxiety are not uncommon after a myocardial infarction, and that treating it leads to better outcomes.[15] As a result, along with amazing strides in understanding the biology of disease, the medical field has seen growth in the psychosocial understanding of disease. Academic medical centers, for example, have established divisions for complementary treatments. Our medical colleagues would rarely prescribe an antihypertensive medication in the twenty-first century without counseling patients on the need for good diet and exercise. Referrals to nutritionists, personal trainers, and other wellness experts are routine. Why should the addictions field settle for less? Long gone should be the days of patients with addictions being treated with anything less than first-rate treatments in first-rate facilities. Just as we do not help our patients when we see addictions as issues of moral weakness, we also do them a disservice if we focus only on medications and brain receptors. Ours is a society overfocused on these things. When you watch your baseball or basketball team on television you will be reminded many times that you need a pill to enhance your sexual performance. Who needs to work on the relationship? Take the pill, and all will be well. Our addicted patients take this mentality to the extreme. Handed a genetic disposition at conception, they have perfected the use of pills "to make it all better."

We have a lot of catching up to do. A biological understanding is where the rest of medicine was a decade or two ago. They have moved on, and we need to run to catch up. Of course we do have the advantage of having developed good psychosocial understandings and treatments of addictive disorders. Integrating these as we jog forward will be crucial. In the next chapter we will discuss this integrated treatment approach.

How the SMH Can Guide
Treatment and Recovery

The SMH is grounded in the observation that one of the most compelling reasons why individuals become addicted is that a particular drug or behavior changes, relieves, diminishes, or makes more bearable human psychological suffering. Treatments that work should do so because they alleviate the suffering which drives addictive behavior. Although there are few if any silver linings in the way addictive drugs and behaviors have permeated society in epidemic proportions over the past half century, during this same period we have seen encouraging treatments emerge that offer considerable hope for recovery if not cure. New psychological and biological approaches, often best combined, respond to the vulnerabilities which predispose people to addictions. An extensive review of all the treatments for alcoholism and other addictions would go beyond the scope of this book. Here we will briefly discuss how the SMH, and the psychodynamic perspective from which it derives, can guide patients, families, and practitioners to appreciate what can work and why. For our purposes here, the types of treatment can be summarized as self-help, psychotherapeutic, and psychopharmacologic.

SELF-HELP

The best-known and most widely available self-help programs are the twelve-step programs such as Alcoholics Anonymous (AA), Cocaine Anonymous (CA), Narcotics Anonymous (NA), and so forth. Alternative programs such as Smart Recovery have also evolved over the past several decades for those who cannot accept the traditions and culture of twelve-step programs. Until recently it has been difficult to scientifically prove the effectiveness of twelve-step programs because of the anonymous traditions of AA. However, Project MATCH, sponsored by the National Institute of Alcohol Abuse and Alcoholism (NIAAA) has proven it to be an extremely effective intervention.[1] Some would argue that the twelve-step programs work because placing a group emphasis on the requirement of abstinence removes the offending agent and thus assures recovery. In our experience, twelve-step programs work because they use extremely sophisticated group psychology which provides containing and change-producing experiences which address the needs of addictively vulnerable individuals.

One of the most distinguishing features of addiction is the loss of control. It involves not only the loss of control of the substance or behavior, but also the loss of control of one's life. One of the first steps in getting better is acknowledging this reality. AA and related self-help groups are extremely beneficial in helping members appreciate and make this first step.

Contrary to some common misunderstandings, the main requirement of AA is not a belief in God, abstinence, or adherence to any particular credo but the honest desire to stop drinking or drugging. With this simple requirement a person is introduced to a culture which fosters openness, acceptance, helpful guidelines, and encouragement to "not pickup" and to keep coming back. Most importantly, it is a culture which helps individuals to accept that they are powerless over their addiction and that their lives had become unmanageable because of their addiction (i.e., the first step: "We admitted we were powerless over alcohol [drugs] . . . that our lives had become unmanageable"). Rather than tell them that they can never have another drink or drug, AA encourages members to keep it simple and consider not drinking or drugging that day, to "take it one day at a time." Nevertheless, in fostering abstinence the program produces an environment in which as individuals stop use of their addictive substance they often discover that one of the major determinants of the overuse has been removed. Namely, the problem of physical dependence diminishes and the craving or desire for the alcohol recedes. Having removed the physical demand for the use of substances, individuals become better positioned to face the emotional and behavioral dysregulation which precipitated and maintained the addictive behavior. This first step becomes a means then to contain and resist a destructive behavior that was otherwise uncontained and uncontrollable by admitting to having a disease or illness and that they had lost control of their lives.

Beyond the necessary requirements of establishing control at the outset, twelve-step programs are ingenious at helping individuals to change the things about themselves and their situations that made them susceptible to their addiction. The vulnerabilities leading to addiction (i.e., dysregulation of feelings, self-esteem, relationships, and self-care) produce self-defeating defenses and personality characteristics. In the program they refer to these qualities as "character defects." If there is not a degree of self-absorption involved in the development of addictive behavior, addiction certainly fosters or heightens it. Twelve-step programs use storytelling traditions to gradually foster a climate of self-examination and change. The tradition helps participants listen to stories demonstrating that they are not alone in having difficulties in regulating their emotions, self-esteem, relationships, and self-care. Through the stories, people learn about knowing and regulating their feelings, overcoming their guilt, shame, and low self-esteem, and connecting to other human beings. In this respect AA becomes a comforting experience for individuals whose self-regulation difficulties have made them very uncomfortable. The spiritual element of AA helps many who attend meetings with such discomfort. Clearly, AA addresses the spiritual dimension of the person with an alcohol problem, looks at the spiritual component of the disorder's development, and encourages growth in the person's spiritual dimension. The notion of forgiveness, for example, pervade's AA meetings.[2]

The stories in AA also help members recognize in others and themselves the off-putting and self-defeating personality characteristics emanating from these vulnerabilities, which are so much a part of their susceptibility to addiction. Participants come to appreciate that the worst fate in life is not to suffer; rather, the worst fate is to suffer alone. As a consequence, defensive self-sufficiency is replaced with an appreciation for the inescapable interdependence of life. Over time there is a gradual shift from self-absorption to altruism and a genuine caring for and about others. AA challenges the assumptions that we can best govern our lives and take care of ourselves alone.[3]

PSYCHOTHERAPY

An old aphorism from the twelve-step tradition is that people have to hit "rock bottom" before abstinence and recovery can occur. A more contemporary aphorism from the same tradition likens addiction to a person deciding when to get off an elevator that is going down. Most modern psychotherapists do not subscribe to the notion of the inevitable disasters of "bottoming out" as a requirement for recovery. Rather one of the main and initial functions of therapy becomes one of stimulating motivation to acknowledge one's addiction and begin doing something about it.

A number of types of psychotherapy, including individual, group, couples, and family therapy, have developed over the past several decades to treat addictions. Given that addicted individuals are bewildered or overwhelmed by their feelings, that they do not feel good about themselves, that satisfactory relationships are elusive or absent, and that they do not take good care of themselves, effective treatments must respond to these vulnerabilities. Regardless of the type or orientation of the therapy, we believe there are essential elements for the conduct of effective treatment, elements with which most practitioners would agree. We would include the following:

- Kindness
- Comfort
- Empathy
- Patience (remember the problems with alexithymia, action, avoidance)
- Instruction (e.g., help individuals to learn about emotions and self-care)
- Self-awareness (therapist/patient)
- Climate of mutual respect (the therapeutic alliance)
- Balance (talking/listening)

In addition to psychodynamic psychotherapy, the approach with which we are most experienced, there are several others which have proven effective; these include cognitive behavioral therapy (CBT), motivational enhancement therapy (MET), and dialectic behavioral therapy (DBT). Given the self-regulation difficulties with which addicted individuals struggle, effective therapists appreciate the crucial need for a friendly, supportive, and empathic relationship. A premium is placed on fostering comfort; being active, interactive, instructive; and having a willingness to develop a focus—namely on what the important determinants are that precipitate, maintain, and cause relapse to addictive behaviors. From a psychodynamic perspective, supportive-expressive therapy (SET) has proven effective in exploring core relationship problems.[4] In our own

modified psychodynamic approach we have placed the focus on disturbances in regulating emotions, self-esteem, relationships, and self-care.[5]
CBT focuses similarly on interpersonal and intrapersonal perceptions and
experiences, examining the emotions, behaviors, and thinking which precipitate, maintain, and cause relapse.[6] And MET, based on a "stages of
change model,"[7] guides and motivates individuals to overcome their denial
of an addiction (pre-contemplation), to begin to consider that they do
have a problem (contemplation), to ready themselves for change (preparation), to do some things about it (action), and then to sustain their recovery (maintenance). This approach rests on a foundation of empathy, support for self-efficacy, avoiding arguments, yielding to resistance, and
pursuing discrepancies in what patients do and say.[8] In our opinion, therapists wittingly and unwittingly combine in practice aspects of each of
these approaches, although some might protest that they strictly adhere to
one of these models. These therapies access and modify the vulnerabilities
which cause addicted persons so much of their distress. They can significantly ameliorate the distress which individuals try to medicate with addictive substances and behaviors.

In our work we have been especially impressed with the beneficial aspects of group psychotherapy. We have developed a modified dynamic
group therapy (MDGT) for substance abusers that effectively focuses on
and alters the problems with experiencing and expressing emotions, self-
esteem, relationships, and self-care—the major underpinnings of addictions and the distress which individuals try to self-medicate with addictive
substances and behaviors.[9]

Groups contain and they transform. Beyond providing contain-
ment, perhaps more importantly, groups play a crucial role in trans-
forming behavior—particularly character styles and behavior patterns
that predispose people to addictive behavior. Patients help each other focus on safety and survival requirements, especially given their problems
with behavioral and emotional dysregulation. In their group interactions
patients naturally express fear, apprehension, and anxiety about each
other in life-threatening situations. They provide nonjudgmental pro-
scription of behavior and evoke appropriate alarm regarding self-care
lapses which might herald a relapse to drugs. With a trained leader
groups can stimulate processes which go beyond matters of safety and
support. Groups are excellent forums to foster self-examination, especially in the domain of feelings and the characterologic defenses and behaviors that sometimes mask them. They provide powerful antidotes for

problems with self-esteem, foster effective connection with others, and facilitate a process to examine how and why individuals operate to make such connections unlikely or impossible.[10]

As we mentioned at the beginning of this book, the suffering and bewilderment with the addictive process impacts not only the person with the illness, but also all of those who come into his or her orbit—family, friends, colleagues. In recent decades, support groups, such as Al Anon, have evolved to help these people better understand and respond to the dysfunctional relationship that exists between the person with an addiction and his or her object of addiction.

MEDICATION

Not so long ago, medication interventions were frequently considered mutually exclusive with non-medication interventions. Numerous studies, however, have demonstrated that medication and non-medication interventions are complementary, and when combined, typically yield better results. For example, McLellan and colleagues studied the effects of adding different amounts of treatment services to a methadone treatment for a large group of people with opiate dependence. They found that the group that did best received the greatest variety of services, such as family therapy and employment counseling.[11] Similarly, addictions patients with comorbid psychiatric disorders do better when they receive integrated treatment for both disorders. For example, Weiss and associates have treated substance-dependent bipolar people with integrated group therapy (IGT) and found that IGT patients had better outcomes on several measures, including percentage of months abstinent.[12]

If a person is physically dependent on a substance, treatment usually begins with detoxification. There are a variety of medical detoxification strategies for alcohol, opioids, and sedative-hypnotics such as the benzodiazepines. Whichever strategy is used, the relapse rate is virtually 100 percent if detoxification is not followed by further treatment.

Medications have been developed for maintaining abstinence for people with alcohol disorders and opioid disorders. Disulfiram (antabuse) prevents the complete metabolism of alcohol. If a person drinks alcohol after taking disulfiram, the noxious metabolite acetaldehyde builds up in the body, resulting in an unpleasant reaction, including nausea and vomiting. The medication naltrexone (Revia) blocks the opioid mu receptors in the brain. As we saw in chapter 12, this prevents the endogenous opioids released by the ingestion of alcohol from binding to receptors in the reward pathway, preventing the release of dopamine. Thus one of the rewarding brain effects of alcohol ingestion is eliminated. Finally, acamprosate (Campral) seems to work by diminishing the effects of the brain's glutamate neurotransmitter system. This system is the brain's major "excitatory" neurotransmitter system and is especially active during the phase of alcohol withdrawal.

Methadone is one of the medications available to treat opioid dependence. As noted above, this medication, like all addictions medications, is meant to be prescribed in the context of comprehensive psychosocial services. In fact, it can only be prescribed for opioid dependence by licensed and accredited opioid treatment programs that provide counseling and other services. Methadone is an opioid receptor agonist. That is, it acts like the endogenous opioids at the brain receptors where these endorphins have their action. Methadone prevents withdrawal and craving and blocks the effects of other opioids. While it can be abused, when provided appropriately in the context of a licensed and accredited program, decades of research have shown that it results in decreased substance abuse, less criminal behavior, and a return to activities such as work and family life.[13] Often a hot-button topic of ideological arguments, methadone is frequently criticized as a replacement addiction. Leaving ideology aside, we can say that we have both worked with methadone patients, and our experience reflects what the research has shown: this has been a life-saving intervention.

Another option for people with opioid dependence is buprenorphine (Suboxone and Subutex). Like methadone, it acts at the mu opioid receptors to prevent withdrawal and craving. Unlike methadone, however, it is a *partial* agonist, which is active at the receptors up to a certain point, then has no more additional activity, but still acts to block the receptors. In the Suboxone preparation, buprenorphine is compounded with naloxone, a mu receptor antagonist or blocker. This formulation was developed to address the temptation of injecting the buprenorphine to get some additional effect. In fact, the antagonist naltrexone (Revia) is the third option for treatment of opioid dependence. Again, the antagonists block the opioid receptors to prevent drugs such as heroin from reaching these receptors.

There are also medications approved for the treatment of nicotine dependence—the antidepressant bupropion, for example, as well as a variety of nicotine replacement preparations, and, more recently, varenicline

(Chantix), a nicotine receptor partial agonist. While various medications have been tried and are currently under investigation for treatment of other SUDs, such as cocaine dependence, nothing has yet been approved by the Food and Drug Administration. Similarly, while no medication is approved per se for both sets of disorders in dual diagnosis patients, many medications—mainly antidepressants, antipsychotics, and mood stabilizers—have been shown to be safe and effective for the psychiatric disorder in people with SUDs. This is important because the psychiatric disorders are a source of distress that helps drive the SUD. Similarly, we have observed that addictions medications such as methadone and Suboxone, from a self-medication perspective, provide stabilizing relief not only from physical discomfort, but also from psychological distress. This is similar to the way they discovered, in the short term, that using heroin and other nonprescribed opiates relieved their distress, although it was destabilizing in the long run.

In the end, we view medications as a beginning to treatment, rather than as the end. They provide a foot in the door, if you will. By helping to ease the discomfort that both predisposes to substance use and results from it, the medications remove the preoccupation with getting and using substances. In doing so, they allow people to participate actively in the other forms of treatment—such as individual, family, or group counseling— meant to address the variety of issues evolving from the dysregulation in their lives. The following case illustrates how we combine medication and psychosocial treatment:

Loretta

Loretta is a thirty-five-year-old single mother of two young sons. Her younger son has severe anxiety and learning difficulties. Although she had had periods of binge drinking and some experimentation with marijuana during adolescence, she had no other history of substance use. After a minor surgical procedure, she was prescribed an opiate pain medication for post-operative pain. She found that the medication relieved not only the physical pain, but also the emotional distress that she had been unaware was so prevalent in her life, especially stemming from the intense level of care required by her younger son. Initially, the pain medication helped her attend to her activities without feeling quite so stressed. Soon, however, she started to escalate her use, and was cut off by her medical providers, with instructions to seek addictions treatment. For a while, she bought pain medications on the street. Her out-of-control use, however, resulted in her losing her job in a middle school cafeteria. Also, she fell into a pat-

tern of not getting her sons to school on time, which brought her to the attention of their elementary school principal. Confronted, she agreed to enter a detoxification program. She was discharged on Suboxone and was referred to an outpatient addictions program.

On the Suboxone, she reported feeling "comfortable and normal for the first time ever!" After a couple of months of sobriety, it became clear that she suffered from major depression, which had never been diagnosed. She was started on an antidepressant, with good effect. Loretta was referred to a group for opiate-dependent people. There she started to address some of the self-care issues that she "had never been very good at taking care of." When that finished, because she continued to have difficulty with her special needs son, she was referred to a woman's group which focused on parenting issues. Through participating in discussions about the shared experiences of the group, she has developed skills to more effectively deal with the stressors that "used to make me want to use." She has returned to work. Over the course of treatment, interestingly, she went from feeling comfortable, to wondering how much less stressed she might feel if she went back to using pain medications, to how much better off she and her sons were because of the sobriety and the skills she was learning through treatment.

In Loretta's case, the Suboxone served to keep her comfortable enough to allow her to keep coming back for the treatment she needed to address several issues in her life. In addition, by helping her to maintain sobriety, her addictions treatment allowed her clinicians to diagnose her depression and treat it, thus addressing another major contributor to her drive to use substances.

OTHER TREATMENT ISSUES

Over the past couple of decades, more attention has been paid to a patient's motivation to change his or her addictive behavior. Much has been written about matching treatment interventions to the motivational stage of the person. For example, people who are not convinced that they have an addiction problem are considered to be at a *precontemplative* or *contemplative* stage. A sensible treatment intervention would be to engage the person in a dialogue about the pros and cons of ongoing substance use. A recommendation to attend a self-help meeting, while perhaps appropriate for somebody at an *action* stage, probably would not be well received by someone still unsure that they have a problem. Certainly, in our approach to patients we make an effort to tailor treatment interventions to their motivational stages.

It is also important to consider the role of what we refer to as nonspecific treatment factors.[14] Frequently these factors involve the qualities of the treatment provider and the relationship she establishes with the patient. The contribution of these nonspecific factors was evident to us when we recently reviewed the results of a study investigating the efficacy of a medication called topiramate for people with alcohol dependence.[15] Half the patients received topiramate, and half received a placebo. While the topiramate patients did better, everybody improved—a tribute to the behavioral treatment, which was provided to everybody. Intriguingly, however, the largest drinking reduction during the course of the study was seen between the screening and enrollment periods. Thus, even before anybody swallowed their first pill—topiramate or placebo—they were making big changes in drinking behavior. This probably had a lot to do with a concerned professional engaging them in a thoughtful discussion (i.e., the screening process) that heightened awareness of the drinking problem in a non-judgmental way.

UNASSISTED RECOVERY

Some people do recover from addictions without treatment. In fact, this may be more common than expected. Those who experience unassisted recovery tend to have milder forms of their disorder, and fewer coexisting problems that complicate the recovery process.[16]

This as an exciting time to be an addictions treatment provider, and an opportune time for those suffering with addictions, because there are a variety of effective treatment interventions—medication and non-medication—that we can use to address the spectrum of difficulties encountered by our patients with SUDs, both with and without psychiatric disorders. It is not an exaggeration to say that the SMH anticipated the development of the array of treatments by focusing on the underlying issues contributing to ongoing substance use and abuse. While the SMH has directly spawned the development of MDGT, it encourages investigation—both in the brain and in the person—of the dysregulation underlying addiction. Similarly, by paying better attention to the relationship between poor self-regulation and addiction, we are always alert for affective, interpersonal, self-care, and self-esteem difficulties, and in a better position to offer our patients guidance about what family, group, individual, and medication treatments might be helpful.

· *14* ·

Conclusion

$\mathscr{T}$he bewildering and devastating nature of addictive behavior begs for understanding. It begs for understanding for those who experience it, witness it, study it, and treat it. Addictions are enslaving. The self-medication hypothesis is a compassionate model for providing understanding, hope, and treatment—factors which can liberate those who suffer with it. Models can limit, but their guidance is necessary in solving complex problems such as addictive disorders. We have made a case in this book for the ways in which the SMH provides a humanistic psychological understanding for addictive behavior, one which sees people with addictions as a fundamentally vulnerable population. It is an understanding which counters the horrific judgments and stigmas addicts place upon themselves, to say nothing of similar or harsher judgments others place on them. Furthermore, addictions evoke alternating reactions of concern and intolerance in family and friends who live with and witness the problem. It is our hope that the perspective offered here may provide a measure of restraint, understanding, and hope in dealing with it.

Although addictions clearly have a biological basis and have features resembling a physical disease, we have presented extensive clinical and scientific evidence indicating that it is just as much a disorder rooted in psychological and psychiatric vulnerabilities, which make addictive substances and behaviors so powerfully seductive and consuming. Albeit more often doomed to fail, addictive substances and behaviors are attempts at self-correction for individuals who are often unable to find alternative solutions. We have tried to address what it is that individuals are wittingly and unwittingly trying to correct. For some it seems feelings are too intense or the capacity to bear them is limited and addictive drugs and behaviors provide relief or protection against what otherwise seems unendurable. For others the motive for resorting to addictive solutions seems to be a need to counter confusing and unnameable emotions by changing them through addictive actions and drugs, even if they endure more pain for the choice. For yet others addictive drugs temporarily boost self-esteem and confidence and make contact and relationships with others more likely when otherwise human relationships seem hazardous or impossible. And all this is heightened or compounded by poorly developed capacities for self-care, which makes the risky behaviors associated with addiction more likely.

The SMH of addiction is rooted in the inner experience of those who suffer and endure it. The model relies on the narrative traditions of psychodynamic and clinical psychiatry. It tries to appreciate as well the contributions that genetic and biologic factors make in the development of these disorders.[1] At the same time, we try not to ignore the disabling social and economic factors that loom in the foreground and background in the development of addictive disorders. We have always maintained that the SMH approach should be considered in parallel with other approaches and not in competition with them. Our respected colleague, Dr. Jesse Suh, also provides the empirical evidence in chapter 4 that our clinical data, on which the SMH is primarily based, is validated by his own work and the work of many other clinical and scientific investigators.

It is noteworthy that emotional experiences which are extremely daunting and painful, whether they are intensely threatening feelings unto themselves or the pain of psychiatric conditions such as PTSD, bipolar illness, depression, schizophrenia, or panic disorders, are circumstances disproportionately associated with substance use disorders. When individuals burdened with such problems medicate themselves with addictive substances, it is less the intention to derive pleasure or self-destruction, but more to find cessation or relief from unendurable suffering and pain in the absence of alternatives.

The suffering associated with these aspects of addictive behavior is not sufficiently voiced by those who experience addiction, nor is it sufficiently appreciated by those who witness, treat, or study addiction. By asking not "What do substances do *to* you?" but "What do substances do *for* you?" the self medication model has given voice to a new dialogue on addiction. Our patients and their stories provide a basis to explain how and why their addictions were solutions, at least in the short term, as much as the solutions were a problem. Some have expressed concern that people might use the SMH as a rationale to continue using substances.[2] We would suggest that the problem is not with the SMH, but with people who misinterpret it. In our experience, far from looking for an excuse to continue using, most of our patients beat themselves up mercilessly with every slip or relapse.

When addictions are active they put on a gruesome face and exhibit an incomprehensible voice. It is our hope that this book has given a more humane face and a more understandable voice to those who suffer with addictive disorders. It is also intended to provide a more encouraging face and voice for those who witness, study, and treat it—a face and voice that is restorative and healing, for all the vulnerabilities and painful consequences involved in the addictions.

Afterword

The Self Medication Hypothesis: A Proven Approach to Understanding Addiction

$\mathcal{T}$he self medication hypothesis (SMH) of addiction—originated by Khantzian, Albanese, and their colleagues over thirty years ago—has made a particularly strong contribution to clinical understanding and research direction in addiction. However, over the decades since the SMH was developed there have been remarkable research discoveries in the basic biology of addiction, leading to new medications, therapies, and interventions for addictive disorders. Thus, it is fair to ask whether this important historical contribution to the understanding and treatment of addiction is still relevant today. The brief answer is a definitive yes, and this new book incorporates not only a proven and now longstanding theory, but also the latest research in the field into a useful and comprehensive guide for the addicted, their loved ones, and clinical practitioners.

Even a cursory listing of some of the more significant scientific advances over the past thirty years shows how much has changed in our understanding of addiction. For example, when SMH was first developed we had no knowledge about the actions of alcohol, opiates, cocaine, marijuana, or other addictive drugs on neurological function. Indeed, the study of addictive drugs can be credited with contributing to the identification of specific classes of nerve receptors and to our still fundamental understanding of receptor function. Tolerance and withdrawal were well characterized in a clinically descriptive sense, but there was no clear understanding of the neurochemical mechanisms behind those phenomena. While it is safe to say that most clinical workers in addiction during the 1970s would have bet that the repeated use of high doses of addictive drugs caused specific and long-lasting brain changes, the physics of CAT, PET, MRI, or FMRI had not been invented to help describe and define the anatomy and physiology of those changes. While there was suspicion that some addictive disorders were inherited, in the early 1970s there was no ability to do the sub-molecular biology and chemistry necessary to identify specific genes associated with vulnerability to various addictions. Finally, and related to the dearth of scientific information about addiction, there was actually very little agreement that addiction was an illness at all. Indeed, addiction was widely considered simply a bad habit and an indication of a personal character flaw. Thus, it is not surprising that the SMH was one of the very few efforts to *treat* addiction. Besides AA for alcoholics, therapeutic communities for drug-dependent individuals, and a few thirty-day, residential chemical dependency programs—all developed by and for the benefit of addicted people themselves—the scientific and medical communities had very little to offer in the way of therapeutic methods or modalities for the treatment of addictions.

But much has changed, and for the better, during the past thirty years in the field of addiction. For example, there is now a large and active medical society dedicated to the training and promotion of physician involvement in the treatment of addiction (American Society on Addiction Medicine). There also is an active psychiatric organization, the American Academy of Addiction Psychiatry (AAAP), dedicated to fostering psychiatric expertise and involvement in understanding and treating addiction. Pharmaceutical firms have developed and are in the active marketing stage with more than a dozen new medications to treat nicotine, marijuana, alcohol, cocaine, and opioid (but still not amphetamine) addictions. Technological developments in brain imaging, molecular biology, and genetics are producing new and important understandings about addiction—literally every day.

These findings have already translated into a new level of understanding about the way society deals with addiction disorders. Addictions are increasingly being understood as chronic illnesses requiring extended care, monitoring, and supports. The criminal justice system has developed over 1,500 drug courts where offenders charged with drug-related crimes can receive treatment in the context of judicial supervision, instead of simply incarceration. And primary care physicians, who until very recently had essentially no involvement with addiction, are now screening, doing brief interventions with, and providing medications for their patients with alcohol and drug use disorders.

With this rapidly developing scientific and technological base, do we still need the SMH of addiction—and if so, for what? My answers, described in more detail below, are "absolutely" and "to provide the understanding and perspective that society, families, and addicted individuals themselves need to deal with addiction."

SMH AND THE SOCIETAL VIEW OF ADDICTION AS HEDONISM

Most of society fears addiction and loathes those who fall prey to it. There is, of course, objective reason for this loathing, as abuse of alcohol and other drugs is behind many contemporary threats to public health and safety. However, beyond these objective reasons is a subjective disgust for addiction, based upon the view that addictive behavior is simply wanton pleasure seeking. In our society, responsibility is important and those who abandon social and family responsibilities in the pursuit of personal pleasure are held in particularly low regard. Thus, in this context, strong and swift punishment of addictive behaviors has been a natural response; and the idea of providing treatment and supports to addicted individuals has not been acceptable.

I think one of the more important and continuing contributions of the SMH is in helping society to understand the destructive behaviors associated with addiction and to support a therapeutic approach to this problem. The SMH provides a framework that allows for both societal sanctioning of addictive behaviors and treatment of the underlying personal problems of those who are addicted. Thanks to the clinical observations and research studies fostered by the SMH, there is ample indication of the loneliness, depression, anxiety, and continuing effects of early trauma that affect the great majority of these "hedonistic" individuals. This realization makes it politically possible for society to see beyond what appear to be the purely hedonistic drug-seeking behaviors of addicted individuals. In turn, this changed societal reactions to addiction from purely "law and order" to a more complex and nuanced understanding that punishment alone will not produce the hoped-for life lesson or epiphany that will reduce relapse and re-addiction. Even—and perhaps especially— among those within the judicial and criminal justice systems, there is now recognition that the most severely addicted individuals need more than punishment and more than simply treatment for the obvious signs and symptoms of their addiction. As indicated above, this understanding has contributed to the development of an active addiction treatment system within the correctional fields, to the development of drug and DWI courts and to treatment as a stipulated condition of probation and parole.

SMH AND THE DEVELOPMENT OF EXTENDED TREATMENTS FOR ADDICTION

Beyond providing the general context for society to understand and develop policies to deal with addiction, the SMH continues to provide specific and powerful clinical insights and options for treating this illness. Despite the scientific advances associated with the study of addiction to alcohol and other drugs, within the addiction treatment field, there continues to be what I think is a disturbingly narrow focus upon the exclusive treatment of the signs and symptoms of addiction. This focus has produced improved methods to reduce the discomfort of withdrawal and to provide chemical protections against the direct effects of some drugs. Of course, these treatments are important and necessary, but like the authors of this book, I think they are not adequate. As the authors say:

> The mechanisms of withdrawal and tolerance are insufficient alone to explain the powerful, compelling, and consuming course of addictive illness, and biological mechanisms on their own cannot explain relapse after a person has established abstinence for years.

In this context, one special contribution of the SMH is that it helps both clinician and patient understand that there will be continued vulnerability to drug use well beyond the disappearance of physical signs and symptoms. The SMH also gives specific indications regarding the kinds of emotional and environmental states that are likely to provide the most significant sources of that vulnerability. As noted by the authors:

> Lethargic individuals who might be depressed welcome the energizing and activating effects of a stimulant drug such as cocaine or "speed."
>
> The hyperactive person benefits from the paradoxical calming effects of stimulants. A person who is uptight and uncomfortable about expressing emotion might find repeated low to moderate doses of alcohol appealing because he/she briefly can tolerate such feelings.

Higher doses of alcohol may be required to quiet down those who are more extremely tense, anxious or agitated. And for those who become agitated, angry and rageful, opiates provide calming and comforting influence.

Two clinically important implications follow from these clinically validated and widely replicated observations. First, the underlying emotional and relationship problems of addicted individuals will *not* be adequately addressed with the thirty to sixty days that insurance companies and state treatment policies now typically support. In turn, these enduring emotional problems will provide an important vulnerability to relapse. A second implication from the SMH is that many to most relapses are both specific and predictable—but not generic. That is, the SMH provides predictive clinical specificity in the treatment of an individual. This predictive power comes from a deep understanding of the *specific* relationships found in individual patients between their particular drug preferences; and the specific emotional, environmental and relationship contexts that will make them most vulnerable to relapse. Some of these emotional states (depression) and environments (a bar or a drug-saturated neighborhood) are generic sources of vulnerability. However, many sources of particular vulnerability in an individual patient can be determined only when a clinician understands the core emotional and relationship problems of an individual patient and the specific, if temporary, benefits derived from use of a particular drug in the context of those problem states. In turn, this predictive power can provide the legitimacy and clinical authority necessary to help a patient understand these internal and external vulnerabilities, and the foundation for a longer-term clinical strategy toward the development of patient self-management.

CONTINUING ROLE FOR SMH?

In my view, the SMH is still a viable and indeed necessary context for the treatment of addiction. While we do *not* yet have a cure for severe addictions, we *do* have effective clinical strategies for managing addiction over the long term. Virtually all of these strategies can trace their foundations to the general compassion and specific clinical methods originally suggested by the SMH of addiction. There are few theories or clinical contributions in any field that have lasted over thirty years. Even fewer continue to provide both a general framework for understanding as well as specific clinical strategies for addressing an illness or disease. Regardless of whether you are an addiction treatment professional, the family member of an addicted person, or an affected individual, reading this book should provide a fundamental psychological understanding of addiction as well as insights into some of the complex, puzzling, and self-destructive effects of addictive illness.

> A. Thomas McLellan
> Chief Executive Officer
> Treatment Research Institute
> Philadelphia, PA

Notes

INTRODUCTION

1. R. Glass, "Blue Mood, Blackened Lungs: Depression and Smoking," *Journal of the American Medical Association* 264 (1990): 1259–1264.

2. R. I. Solomon, "The Opponent-Process Theory of Acquired Motivation," *American Psychologist* 35 (1980): 691–712; G. F. Koob, A. Markou, F. Weiss, et al., "Opponent Process and Drug Dependence: Neurobiological Mechanisms," *Seminars in Neuroscience* 5 (1993): 351–358.

3. E. J. Khantzian, "The Self-Medication Hypothesis of Substance Use Disorders: A Reconsideration and Recent Applications," *Harvard Review of Psychiatry* 4 (1997): 231–244.

CHAPTER 1: WHY THE SELF-MEDICATION HYPOTHESIS?

1. Mary Nada, "Mary Nada: From the Beginning, a Passionate Voice for Vineyard House," *Vineyard House News* 9 (2007): 6. This quote is by a member of the board of directors of Vineyard House, a sober house on the Island of Martha's Vineyard in Massachusetts, a program with which one of us (EJK) is proudly affiliated. The House has been an extraordinarily beneficial and restorative resource. Mary has dedicated a great deal of her life to helping individuals who have succumbed to addictive disorders. She knows firsthand the heartbreak of addiction, having witnessed it in a family member who now helps others in their rehabilitation. She also knows the miracle and hope of recovery and offers this sensitive and insightful explanation of what addictive vulnerability is about.

2. R. C. Kessler, P. Berglund, O. Demler, R. Jin, and E. E. Walters, "Lifetime Prevalence and Age-of-Onset Distributions of DSM-IV Disorders in the

National Comorbidity Survey Replication," *Archives of General Psychiatry* 62 (2005): 593–602.

3. M. Szalavitz, "So What Made Me an Addict?" *Washington Post*, August 28, 2007.

CHAPTER 2: ADDICTION: DISEASE OR DISORDER

1. B. A. van der Kolk, A. C. McFarlane, and L. Weisaeth, *Traumatic Stress* (New York: Guilford Press, 1996).

2. P. Ouimette and P. J. Brown, eds., *Trauma and Substance Abuse: Causes, and Consequences, and Treatment of Comorbid Disorders* (Washington, DC: American Psychological Association, 2003).

3. J. D. Swendsen, H. Tennen, M. L. Carney, et al., "Mood and Alcohol Consumption: An Experience Sampling Test of the Self-Medication Hypothesis," *Journal of Abnormal Psychology* 109, no. 2 (2000): 198–204.

4. Personal communication.

CHAPTER 3: THE SMH AND ADDICTION AS A PROBLEM IN SELF-REGULATION

1. P. E. Sifneos, "Clinical Observations on Some Patients Suffering from a Variety of Psychosomatic Diseases," in *Proceedings of the Seventh European Conference on Psychosomatic Research*, ed. S. Karger (Basel, 1967).

2. H. Kohut and E. S. Wolfe, "The Disorders of the Self and Their Treatment," *International Journal of Psychoanalysis* 59 (1978): 413–425.

3. P. J. Flores, *Addiction as an Attachment Disorder* (Lanham, Md.: Jason Aronson, 2004).

4. E. J. Khantzian and J. E. Mack, "Self-Preservation and the Care of the Self—Ego Instincts Reconsidered," *Psychoanalytic Study of the Child* 38 (1983): 209–232.

5. M. P. Paulus, S. F. Tapert, and M. A. Schuckit, "Neural Activation Patterns of Methamphetamine-Dependent Subjects during Decision Making Predict Relapse," *Archives of General Psychiatry* 62 (2005): 761–768.

CHAPTER 4: SELF-MEDICATION HYPOTHESIS RESEARCH: STUDY OF AFFECT REGULATION AND DRUG PREFERENCE

1. J. J. Suh, S. Ruffins, C. E. Robins, M. J. Albanese, and E. J. Khantzian, "Self-Medication Hypothesis: Connecting Affective Experience and Drug

Choice," *Psychoanalytic Psychology* 2008, in press; E. J. Khantzian, "Understanding Addictive Vulnerability," *Neuro-Psychoanalysis* 5 (2003): 5–21.

2. A. Wilson, S. D. Passik, J. Faude, J. Abrams, and E. Gordon, "A Hierarchical Model of Opiate Addiction: Failures of Self-Regulation as a Central Aspect of Substance Abuse." *Journal of Nervous and Mental Disease* 177 (1989): 390–399.

3. S. J. Blatt, W. Berman, S. Bloom-Feshbach, A. Sugarman, C. Wilber, and H. D. Kleber, "Psychological Assessment of Psychopathology in Opiate Addicts," *Journal of Nervous and Mental Disease* 172 (1984): 156–165.

4. J. Foote, M. Seligman, S. Magura, L. Handelsman, A. Rosenblum, M. Lovejoy, K. Arrington, and B. Stimmel, "An Enhanced Positive Reinforcement Model for the Severely Impaired Cocaine Abuser," *Journal of Substance Abuse Treatment* 11 (1994): 525–539.

5. D. M. Fergusson, M. T. Lynskey, and L. J. Horwood, "Comorbidity between Depressive Disorders and Nicotine Dependence in a Cohort of 16-year-olds," *Archives of General Psychiatry* 53 (1996): 1043–1047.

6. J. Shedler and J. Block. "Adolescent Drug Use and Psychological Health: A Longitudinal Inquiry," *American Psychologist* 45 (1990): 612–630.

7. M. A. Southam-Gerow and P. C. Kendall, "Emotion Regulation and Understanding: Implications for Child Psychopathology and Therapy," *Clinical Psychology Review* 22 (2002): 189–222; N. Eisenberg, C. Champion, and Y. Ma, "Emotion-Related Regulation: An Emerging Construct," *Merrill-Palmer Quarterly* 50 (2004): 236–59; J. J. Campos, C. B. Frankel, and L. Camras, "On the Nature of Emotion Regulation," *Child Development* 75 (2004): 377–394.

8. M. Gilliom, D. S. Shaw, J. E. Beck, M. A. Schonberg, and J. L. Lukon, "Anger Regulation in Disadvantaged Preschool Boys: Strategies, Antecedents, and the Development of Self-Control," *Developmental Psychology* 38 (2002): 222–235.

9. J. Garber, N. Braafladt, and B. Weiss, "Affect Regulation in Depressed and Nondepressed Children and Young Adolescents," *Development and Psychopathology* 7 (1995): 93–115; R. Kobak and R. Ferenz-Giles, "Emotion Regulation and Depressive Symptoms during Adolescence: A Functionalist Perspective," *Development and Psychopathology* 7 (1995): 183–192.

10. L. J. Lengua, "The Contribution of Emotionality and Self-Regulation to the Understanding of Children's Response to Multiple Risk," *Child Development* 73 (2002): 144–161; W. Kliewer, J. N. Cunningham, R. Diehl, K. A. Parrish, J. M. Walker, C. Atiyeh, B. Neace, L. Duncan, K. Taylor, and R. Mejia, "Violence Exposure and Adjustment in Inner-city Youth: Child and Caregiver Emotion Regulation Skill, Caregiver-Child Relationship Quality, and Neighborhood Cohesion as Protective Factor," *Journal of Clinical Child and Adolescent Psychology* 33 (2004): 477–487; C. A. Stifter, T. L. Spinrad, and J. M. Braungart-Rieker, "Toward a Developmental Model of Child Compliance: The Role of Emotion Regulation in Infancy," *Child Development* 70 (1999): 21–32.

11. N. Eisenberg, R. A. Fabes, I. K. Guthrie, and M. Reiser, "Dispositional Emotionality and Regulation: Their Role in Predicting Quality of Social Functioning," *Journal of Personality and Social Psychology* 78 (2000): 136–157.

12. B. D. Miller and B. L. Wood, "Influence of Specific Emotional States on Autonomic Reactivity and Pulmonary Function in Asthmatic Children," *Journal of the American Academy of Child and Adolescent Psychiatry* 36 (1997): 669–677; B. Hagekull and G. Bohlin, "Predictors of Middle Childhood Psychosomatic Problems: An Emotion Regulation Approach," *Infant and Child Development* 13 (2004): 389–405.

13. J. J. Gross, and O. P. John, "Individual Differences in Two Emotion Regulation Processes: Implications for Affect, Relationships, and Well-being," *Journal of Personality and Social Psychology* 85 (2003): 348–362; J. J. Gross and R. W. Levenson, "Hiding Feelings: The Acute Effects of Inhibiting Negative and Positive Emotion," *Journal of Abnormal Psychology* 106 (1997): 95–103; G. A. Bonanno, A. Papa, K. Lalande, M. Westphal, and K. Coifman, "The Importance of Being Flexible: The Ability to Both Enhance and Suppress Emotional Expression Predicts Long-term Adjustment," *Psychological Science* 15 (2004): 482–487.

14. E. E. Forbes, A. Miller, J. F. Cohn, N. A. Fox, and M. Kovacs, "Affect-Modulated Startle in Adults with Childhood-onset Depression: Relations to Bipolar Course and Number of Lifetime Depressive Episodes," *Psychiatry Research* 134 (2005): 11–25.

15. J. Rottenberg, F. H. Wilhelm, J. J. Gross, and I. H. Gotlib, "Respiratory Sinus Arrhythmia as a Predictor of Outcome in Major Depressive Disorder," *Journal of Affective Disorders* 71 (2002): 265–272; A. S. Chambers and J. J. Allen, "Vagal Tone as an Indicator of Treatment Response in Major Depression," *Psychophysiology* 39 (2002): 861–864.

16. R. E. Dahl, "The Development of Affect Regulation: Bringing Together Basic and Clinical Perspectives," *Annals of the New York Academy of Sciences* 1008 (2003): 183–188.

17. D. B. Clark, L. Kirisci, and H. B. Moss, "Early Adolescent Gateway Drug Use in Sons of Fathers with Substance Use Disorders," *Addictive Behaviors* 23 (1998): 561–566.

18. C. R. Colder and L. Chassin, "Affectivity and Impulsivity: Temperament Risk for Adolescent Alcohol Involvement," *Psychology of Addictive Behaviors* 11 (1997): 83–97.

19. R. E. Tarter, M. Vanyukov, P. Giancola, M. Dawes, T. Blackson, A. Mezzich, and D. B. Clark, "Etiology of Early Age Onset Substance Use Disorder: A Maturational Perspective," *Development and Psychopathology* 11 (1999): 657–683; R. E. Tarter, T. Blackson, J. Brigham, H. Moss, and G. V. Caprara, "The Association between Childhood Irritability and Liability to Substance Use in Early Adolescence: A 2-year Follow-up Study of Boys at Risk for Substance Abuse," *Drug and Alcohol Dependence* 39 (1995): 253–261.

20. A. Eftekhari, A. P. Turner, and M. E. Larimer, "Anger Expression, Coping, and Substance Use in Adolescent Offenders," *Addictive Behaviors* 29 (2004): 1001–1008.

21. T. A. Wills, J. M. Sandy, O. Shinar, and A. Yaeger, "Contributions of Positive and Negative Affect to Adolescent Substance Use. Test of a Bidimensional

Model in a Longitudinal Study," *Psychology of Addictive Behaviors* 13 (1999): 327–338.

22. A. P. Turner, M. E. Larimer, I. G. Sarason, and E. W. Trupin, "Identifying a Negative Mood Subtype in Incarcerated Adolescents: Relationship to Substance Use," *Addictive Behaviors* 30 (2005): 1442–1448.

23. F. A. Thorberg and M. Lyvers, "Negative Mood Regulation (NMR) Expectancies, Mood, and Affect Intensity among Clients in Substance Disorder Treatment Facilities," *Addictive Behaviors* 31 (2005): 811–820; M. L. Cooper, M. Russell, J. B. Skinner, M. R. Frone, and P. Mudar, "Stress and Alcohol Use: Moderating Effects of Gender, Coping, and Alcohol Expectancies," *Journal of Abnormal Psychology* 101 (1992): 139–152; M. L. Cooper, M. R. Frone, M. Russell, and P. Mudar, "Drinking to Regulate Positive and Negative Emotions: A Motivational Model of Alcohol Use," *Journal of Personality and Social Psychology* 69 (1995): 990–1005; J. S. Simons, K. B. Carey, and R. M. Gaher, "Lability and Impulsivity Synergistically Increase Risk for Alcohol-related Problems," *American Journal of Drug and Alcohol Abuse* 30 (204): 685–694.

24. D. Fishbein, C. Hyde, D. Eldreth, E. D. London, J. Matochik, M. Ernst, N. Isenberg, S. Steckley, B. Schech, and A. Kimes, "Cognitive Performance and Autonomic Reactivity in Abstinent Drug Abusers and Nonusers," *Experimental and Clinical Psychopharmacology* 13 (2005): 25–40.

25. Thorberg and Lyvers, "Negative Mood Regulation."

26. A. R. Childress, R. Ehrman, A. T. McLellan, J. MacRae, M. Natale, and C. P. O'Brien, "Can Induced Moods Trigger Drug-related Responses in Opiate Abuse Patients?" *Journal of Substance Abuse Treatment* 11 (1994): 17–23.

27. R. Sinha, D. Catapano, and S. O'Malley, "Stress-induced Craving and Stress Response in Cocaine Dependent Individuals," *Psychopharmacology* 142 (1999): 343–51; R. Sinha, T. Fuse, L. R. Aubin, and S. S. O'Malley, "Psychological Stress, Drug-related Cues and Cocaine Craving," *Psychopharmacology* 152 (2000): 140–148; J. R. McKay, M. J. Rutherford, A. I. Alterman, J. S. Cacciola, and M. R. Kaplan, "An Examination of the Cocaine Relapse Process," *Drug and Alcohol Dependence* 38 (1995): 35–43; J. R. McKay, M. J. Rutherford, J. S. Cacciola, R. Kabasakalian-McKay, and A. I. Alterman, "Gender Differences in the Relapse Experiences of Cocaine Patients," *Journal of Nervous and Mental Disease* 184 (1996): 616–622; R. C. McMahon, "Personality, Stress, and Social Support in Cocaine Relapse Prediction," *Journal of Substance Abuse Treatment* 21 (2001): 77–87; D. Hasin, X. Liu, E. Nunes, S. McCloud, S. Samet, and J. Endicott, "Effects of Major Depression on Remission and Relapse of Substance Dependence," *Archives of General Psychiatry* 59 (2002): 375–380.

28. J. A. Richman, K. W. Zlatoper, J. L. Zackula Ehmke, and K. M. Rospenda, "Retirement and Drinking Outcomes: Lingering Effects of Workplace Stress?" *Addictive Behaviors* 31 (2006): 767–776.

29. F. Aguilar de Arcos, A. Verdejo-Garcia, M. I. Peralta-Ramirez, M. Sanchez-Barrera, and M. Perez-Garcia. "Experience of Emotions in Substance

Abusers Exposed to Images Containing Neutral, Positive, and Negative Affective Stimuli," *Drug and Alcohol Dependence* 78 (2005): 159–167.

30. G. Gerra, B. Baldaro, A. Zaimovic, G. Moi, M. Bussandri, M. A. Raggi, and F. Brambilla, "Neuroendocrine Responses to Experimentally-induced Emotions among Abstinent Opioid-dependent Subjects," *Drug and Alcohol Dependence* 71 (2003): 25–35.

31. Khantzian, "Understanding Addictive Vulnerability"; E. J. Khantzian, "The Self-Medication Hypothesis of Substance Use Disorders: A Reconsideration and Recent Applications," *Harvard Review of Psychiatry* 4 (1997): 231–244; E. J. Khantzian, *Treating Addiction as a Human Process* (Northvale, N.J.: Jason Aronson Press, 1999).

32. A. T. McLellan, A. R. Childress, and G. E. Woody, "Drug Abuse and Psychiatric Disorders: Role of Drug Choice," in *Substance Abuse and Psychopathology*, ed. A. Alterman (New York: Plenum Press, 1985) 137–172.

33. E. J. Khantzian, K. S. Halliday, and W. E. McAuliffe, *Addiction and the Vulnerable Self: Modified Dynamic Group Therapy for Substance Abusers* (New York: Guilford, 1990); H. Wieder and E. H. Kaplan, "Drug Use in Adolescents: Psychodynamic Meaning and Pharmacogenic Effect," *Psychoanalytic Study of the Child* 24 (1969): 399–431.

34. J. V. Spotts and F. C. Shontz, "Drugs and Personality: Dependence of Findings on Method," *American Journal of Drug and Alcohol Abuse* 12 (1986): 355–382.

35. C. E. Dodgen and W. M. Shea, *Substance Use Disorders: Assessment and Treatment* (London: Academic Press, 2000).

36. E. J. Khantzian, "The Self-Medication Hypothesis of Addictive Disorders: Focus on Heroin and Cocaine Dependence," *American Journal of Psychiatry* 142 (1985): 1259–1264.

37. E. J. Khantzian, J. E. Mack, and A. F. Schatzberg, "Heroin Use as an Attempt to Cope: Clinical Observations." *American Journal of Psychiatry* 131 (1974): 160–164.

38. Khantzian, "Self-Medication Hypothesis of Addictive Disorders: Focus on Heroin and Cocaine Dependence"; E. J. Khantzian, "Psychological (Structural) Vulnerabilities and the Specific Appeal of Narcotics," *Annals of the New York Academy of Sciences* 398 (1982): 24–32.

39. D. Hien, L. Cohen, and A. Campbell, "Is Traumatic Stress a Vulnerability Factor for Women with Substance Use Disorders?" *Clinical Psychology Review* 25 (2005): 813–823; H. D. Chilcoat and N. Breslau, "Investigations of Causal Pathways between PTSD and Drug Use Disorders," *Addictive Behaviors* 23 (1998): 827–840. H. D. Chilcoat and N. Breslau, "Posttraumatic Stress Disorder and Drug Disorders: Testing Causal Pathways," *Archives of General Psychiatry* 55 (1998): 913–917.

40. K. Heffernan, M. Cloitre, K. Tardiff, P. M. Marzuk, L. Portera, and A. C. Leon, "Childhood Trauma as a Correlate of Lifetime Opiate Use in Psychiatric Patients," *Addictive Behaviors* 25 (2000): 797–803.

41. H. W. Clark, C. L. Masson, K. L. Delucchi, S. M. Hall, and K. L. Sees, "Violent Traumatic Events and Drug Abuse Severity," *Journal of Substance Abuse Treatment* 20 (2001): 121–127.

42. Childress et al., "Can Induced Moods Trigger Drug-related Responses in Opiate Abuse Patients?"

43. S. J. Blatt, C. McDonald, A. Sugarman, and C. Wilber, "Psychodynamic Theories of Opiate Addiction: New Directions for Research," *Clinical Psychology Review* 4 (1984): 159–189.

44. Suh et al., "Self-Medication Hypothesis: Connecting Affective Experience and Drug Choice."

45. Dodgen and Shea, *Substance Use Disorders*.

46. Khantzian, "The Self-Medication Hypothesis of Substance Use Disorders: A Reconsideration and Recent Applications"; Khantzian, Halliday, and McAuliffe, *Addiction and the Vulnerable Self*; Khantzian, "The Self-Medication Hypothesis of Addictive Disorders: Focus on Heroin and Cocaine Dependence."

47. Khantzian, Halliday, and McAuliffe, *Addiction and the Vulnerable Self*.

48. R. S. Falck, J. Wang, R. G. Carlson, M. Eddy, and H. A. Siegal, "The Prevalence and Correlates of Depressive Symptomatology among a Community Sample of Crack-cocaine Smokers," *Journal of Psychoactive Drugs* 34 (2002): 281–288; B. F. Grant, F. S. Stinson, D. A. Dawson, S. P. Chou, M. C. Dufour, W. Compton, R. P. Pickering, and K. Kaplan, "Prevalence and Co-occurrence of Substance Use Disorders and Independent Mood and Anxiety Disorders: Results from the National Epidemiologic Survey on Alcohol and Related Conditions," *Archives of General Psychiatry* 61 (2004): 807–816.

49. B. F. Grant, "Comorbidity between DSM-IV Drug Use Disorders and Major Depression: Results of a National Survey of Adults," *Journal of Substance Abuse* 7 (1995): 481–497.

50. C. A. Denier, A. K. Thevos, P. K. Latham, and C. L. Randall, "Psychosocial and Psychopathology Differences in Hospitalized Male and Female Cocaine Abusers: A Retrospective Chart Review," *Addictive Behaviors* 16 (1991): 489–496.

51. R. A. Brown, P. M. Monti, M. G. Myers, R. A. Martin, T. Rivinus, M. E. Dubreuil, and D. J. Rohsenow. "Depression among Cocaine Abusers in Treatment: Relation to Cocaine and Alcohol Use and Treatment Outcome," *American Journal of Psychiatry* 155 (1998): 220–225.

52. D. M. McCarthy, K. L. Tomlinson, K. G. Anderson, G. A. Marlatt, and S. A. Brown, "Relapse in Alcohol- and Drug-disordered Adolescents with Comorbid Psychopathology: Changes in Psychiatric Symptoms," *Psychology of Addictive Behaviors* 19 (2005): 28–34.

53. Khantzian, Halliday, and McAuliffe, *Addiction and the Vulnerable Self*.

54. R. J. Dougherty, and N. J. Lesswing, "Inpatient Cocaine Abusers: An Analysis of Psychological and Demographic Variables," *Journal of Substance Abuse Treatment* 6 (1989): 45–47.

55. J. M. Donovan, S. Soldz, H. F. Kelley, and W. E. Penk, "Four Addictions: The MMPI and Discriminant Function Analysis," *Journal of Addictive Diseases* 17 (1998): 41–55.

56. Suh et al., "Self-Medication Hypothesis: Connecting Affective Experience and Drug Choice."

57. Dodgen and Shea, *Substance Use Disorders.*

58. R. Goldberg, *Drugs across the Spectrum,* volume 4 (Belmont, Calif.: Wadsworth, 2003).

59. Khantzian, *Treating Addiction as a Human Process.*

60. E. J. Khantzian and J. E. Mack, "Alcoholics Anonymous and Contemporary Psychodynamic Theory," in *Recent Developments in Alcoholism,* ed. M. Galanter (New York: Plenum, 1989), 67–89.

61. C. E. Isenhart and D. J. Silversmith, "MMPI-2 Response Styles: Generalization to Alcoholism Assessment," *Psychology of Addictive Behaviors* 10 (1996): 15–123.

62. D. M. Eshbaugh, D. J. Tosi, C. N. Hoyt, and M. A. Murphy, "Some Personality Patterns and Dimensions of Male Alcoholics: A Multivariate Description," *A Clinician's Guide to the Personality Profiles of Alcohol and Drug Abusers: Typological Descriptions Using the MMPI,* ed. D. J. Tosi, D. M. Eshbaugh, and M. A. Murphy (Springfield, Ill.: Charles C. Thomas Publisher, 1993), 17–30; C. Wells, D. J. Tosi, D. M. Eshbaugh, and M. A. Murphy, "Comparison and Discrimination of Male and Female Alcoholic and Substance Abusers." *A Clinician's Guide to the Personality Profiles of Alcohol and Drug Abusers: Typological Descriptions Using the MMPI,* ed. D. J. Tosi, D. M. Eshbaugh, and M. A. Murphy (Springfield, Ill.: Charles C. Thomas Publisher, 1993), 63–73.

63. Suh et al., "Self-Medication Hypothesis: Connecting Affective Experience and Drug Choice."

64. Aguilar de Arcos, "Experience of Emotions in Substance Abusers."

65. Suh et al., "Self-Medication Hypothesis: Connecting Affective Experience and Drug Choice."

66. H. C. Breiter, N. L. Etcoff, P. J. Whalen, W. A. Kennedy, S. L. Rauch, R. L. Buckner, M. M. Strauss, S. E. Hyman, and B. R. Rosen, "Response and Habituation of the Human Amygdala during Visual Processing of Facial Expression," *Neuron* 17 (1996): 875–887; H. Garavan, J. C. Pendergrass, T. J. Ross, E. A. Stein, and R. C. Risinger, "Amygdala Response to Both Positively and Negatively Valenced Stimuli," *Neuroreport* 12 (2001): 2779–2783.

67. R. J. Davidson, D. Pizzagalli, J. B. Nitschke, and K. Putnam, "Depression: Perspectives from Affective Neuroscience," *Annual Review of Psychology* 53 (2002): 545–574; L. Pezawas, A. Meyer-Lindenberg, E. M. Drabant, B. A. Verchinski, K. E. Munoz, B. S. Kolachana, M. F. Egan, V. S. Mattay, A. R. Hariri, and D. R. Weinberger, "5-HTTLPR Polymorphism Impacts Human Cingulate-Amygdala Interactions: A Genetic Susceptibility Mechanism for Depression," *Nature Neuroscience* 8 (2005): 828–834; W. C. Drevets, "Prefrontal Cortical-

Amygdalar Metabolism in Major Depression," *Annals of the New York Academy of Sciences* 877 (1999): 614–637; K. N. Ochsner, S. A. Bunge, J. J. Gross, and J. D. Gabrieli, "Rethinking Feelings: An FMRI Study of the Cognitive Regulation of Emotion," *Journal of Cognitive Neuroscience* 14 (2002): 1215–1229; K. N. Ochsner, R. D. Ray, J. C. Cooper, E. R. Robertson, S. Chopra, J. D. Gabrieli, and J. J. Gross, "For Better or for Worse: Neural Systems Supporting the Cognitive Down- and Up-regulation of Negative Emotion," *Neuroimage* 23 (2004): 483–499.

68. Ochsner et al., "Rethinking Feelings"; Ochsner et al., "For Better or for Worse"; K. L. Phan, D. A. Fitzgerald, P. J. Nathan, G. J. Moore, T. W. Uhde, and M. E. Tancer, "Neural Substrates for Voluntary Suppression of Negative Affect: A Functional Magnetic Resonance Imaging Study," *Biological Psychiatry* 57 (2005): 210–219; S. M. Schaefer, D. C. Jackson, R. J. Davidson, G. K. Aguirre, D. Y. Kimberg, and S. L. Thompson-Schill, "Modulation of Amygdalar Activity by the Conscious Regulation of Negative Emotion," *Journal of Cognitive Neuroscience* 14 (2002): 913–921.

69. A. N. Schor, *Affect Regulation and the Origin of the Self: The Neurobiology of Emotional Development* (Hillsdale, N.J.: Lawrence Erlbaum Associates, 1994).

70. W. C. Drevets, "Neuroimaging Studies of Mood Disorders," *Biological Psychiatry* 48 (2000): 813–829.

71. A. R. Childress, P. D. Mozley, W. McElgin, J. Fitzgerald, M. Reivich, and C. P. O'Brien, "Limbic Activation during Cue-induced Cocaine Craving," *American Journal of Psychiatry* 156 (1999): 11–18.

72. R. Sinha, C. Lacadie, P. Skudlarski, R. K. Fulbright, B. J. Rounsaville, T. R. Kosten, and B. E. Wexler, "Neural Activity Associated with Stress-induced Cocaine Craving: A Functional Magnetic Resonance Imaging Study," *Psychopharmacology* 183 (2005): 171–180.

73. M. J. Albanese, E. J. Khantzian, S. L. Murphy, and A. I. Green, "Decreased Substance Use in Chronically Psychotic Patients Treated with Clozapine," *American Journal of Psychiatry* 151 (1994): 780–781; M. J. Albanese and J. J. Suh, "Risperidone in Cocaine-dependent Patients with Comorbid Psychiatric Disorders," *Journal of Psychiatric Practice* 12 (2006): 306–311; D. A. Smelson, M. F. Losonczy, C. W. Davis, M. Kaune, J. Williams, and D. Ziedonis, "Risperidone Decreases Craving and Relapses in Individuals with Schizophrenia and Cocaine Dependence," *Canadian Journal of Psychiatry* 47 (2002): 671–675.

74. H. M. Pettinati, W. Dundon, and C. Lipkin, "Gender Differences in Response to Sertraline Pharmacotherapy in Type A Alcohol Dependence," *American Journal on Addictions* 13 (2004): 236–247.

75. R. J. Craig, "Psychological Functioning of Cocaine Free-basers Derived from Objective Psychological Tests," *Journal of Clinical Psychology* 44 (1988): 599–606; R. L. Greene, A. E. Adyanthaya, R. M. Morse, and L. J. Davis, Jr., "Personality Variables in Cocaine- and Marijuana-dependent Patients," *Journal of Personality Assessment* 61 (1993): 224–230; J. A. Schinka, G. Curtiss, and

J. M. Mulloy, "Personality Variables and Self-Medication in Substance Abuse," *Journal of Personality Assessment* 63 (1994): 413–422; R. Castaneda, H. Lifshutz, M. Galanter, and H. Franco, "Empirical Assessment of the Self-Medication Hypothesis among Dually Diagnosed Inpatients," *Comprehensive Psychiatry* 35 (1994): 180–184; R. D. Weiss, M. L. Griffin, and S. M. Mirin, "Drug Abuse as Self-Medication for Depression: An Empirical Study," *American Journal of Drug and Alcohol Abuse* 18 (1992): 121–129; E. Aharonovich, H. T. Nguyen, and E. V. Nunes, "Anger and Depressive States among Treatment-seeking Drug Abusers: Testing the Psychopharmacological Specificity Hypothesis," *American Journal on Addictions* 10 (2001): 327–334.

76. M. F. Brunette, K. T. Mueser, H. Xie, and R. E. Drake, "Relationships between Symptoms of Schizophrenia and Substance Abuse," *Journal of Nervous and Mental Disease* 185 (1997): 13–20.

77. B. Henwood and D. K. Padgett, "Reevaluating the Self-Medication Hypothesis among the Dually Diagnosed," *American Journal on Addictions* 16 (2007): 160–165.

78. McCarthy et al., "Relapse in Alcohol- and Drug-disordered Adolescents."

CHAPTER 5: CONTEXTS AND MODELS FOR UNDERSTANDING ADDICTION

1. *DSM-IV-TR, Diagnostic and Statistical Manual of Mental Disorders*, 4th edition, text revision (Washington, D.C.: American Psychiatric Association, 2000).

2. A. C. Heath, A. K. Buckholz, P. A. Madden, et al., "Genetic and Environmental Contributions to Alcohol Dependence Risk in a National Twin Sample: Consistency of Findings in Women and Men," *Psychological Medicine* 27 (1997): 1381–396.

3. D. W. Goodwin, "Alcoholism and Genetics: The Sins of the Fathers," *Archives of General Psychiatry* 42 (1985): 171–174.

4. T. C. Blackson, "Temperament: A Salient Correlate of Risk Factors for Alcohol and Drug Abuse," *Drug and Alcohol Dependence* 36 (1994): 205–214.

5. F. Ducci, M. Enoch, C. Hodgkinson, K. Xu, et al. "Interaction between a Functional MAOA Locus and Childhood Sexual Abuse Predicts Alcoholism and Antisocial Personality Disorder in Adult Women," *Molecular Psychiatry*, June 26, 2007, www.nature.com/mp/journal/v13/n3/full/4002034a.html.

6. D. W. Goodwin, *Alcohol and the Writer* (Kansas City: Andrews & McMeel, 1988).

7. S. W. Ahmed, P. J. Bush, F. R. Davidson, and R. J. Iannotti, "Predicting Children's Use and Intentions to Use Abusable Substances" (paper presented at annual meeting of the American Public Health Association, Anaheim, Calif., 1984).

8. R. Jessor and S. L. Jessor, *Problem Behavior and Psychosocial Development: A Longitudinal Study of Youth* (New York: Academic Press, 1977).

9. D. W. Winnicott, "Transitional Objects and Transitional Phenomena," *International Journal of Psycho-Analysis* 34 (1953): 89–97.

10. E. L. Gardiner, "Brain Reward Mechanisms," in *Substance Abuse: A Comprehensive Textbook* (Philadelphia: Lippincott Williams & Williams, 2005).

11. B. Alexander et al., "Opiate Addiction: The Case for an Adaptive Orientation," *Psychological Bulletin* 92 (1982): 367–381. It is noteworthy that Dr. Alexander in his article cited an early theoretical publication of E.J. Khantzian (1974) in which Khantzian proposed that the restrictive conditions of caging and handling were conditions for which the rats were ill equipped instinctively and self-administration of morphine produced relief.

12. D. Morgan et al., "Social Dominance in Monkeys; Dopamine D2 Receptors and Cocaine Self-administration," *Nature Neuroscience* 5 (2002): 169–174.

13. K. Abraham, "The Psychological Relation between Sexuality and Alcoholism," in *Selected Papers of Karl Abraham* (New York: Basic Books, 1964).

14. S. Rado, "The Psychoanalysis of Pharmacothymia," *Psychoanalysis Quarterly* 2 (1933): 1–23: E. Glover, "On the Etiology of Drug Addiction," in *On the Early Development of Mind* (New York: International Universities Press, 1956).

15. E. J. Khantzian, "The Ego, the Self and Opiate Addiction: Theoretical and Treatment Considerations," *International Review of Psycho-Analysis* 5 (1978): 189–198.

16. G. Sashin, personal communication.

17. L. Director, "Encounters with Omnipotence in the Psychoanalysis of Substance Users," *Psychoanalytic Dialogues* 15, no. 4 (2005): 567–586; N. Burton, "Finding the Lost Girls: Multiplicity and Dissociation in the Treatment of Addictions," *Psychoanalytic Dialogues* 15, no. 4 (2005): 587–612; L. M. Dodes, "Addiction, Helplessness, and Narcissistic Rage," *Psychoanalysis Quarterly* 59 (1990): 398–419; Karen B. Walant, *Creating the Capacity for Attachment: Treating Addictions and the Alienated Self* (Northvale, N.J.: Jason Aronson Inc., 1995).

18. M. Weegman and R. Cohen, *The Psychodynamics of Addiction* (London: Whurr Publishers, 2002).

19. E. J. Khantzian, "The Self-Medication Hypothesis of Substance Use Disorders: A Reconsideration and Recent Applications," *Harvard Review of Psychiatry* 4 (1997): 232.

CHAPTER 6: SUFFERING AND SELF-MEDICATION

1. E. J. Khantzian, "The Self-Medication Hypothesis of Addictive Disorders," *American Journal of Psychiatry* 142 (1985): 1259–1264.

2. E. J. Khantzian and C. J. Treece, "Psychodynamics of Drug Dependence: An Overview," *Psychodynamics of Drug Dependence*, research monograph no. 12. (Rockville, Md.: National Institute on Drug Abuse, 1977), 11–25.

3. L. Wurmser, "Psychoanalytic Considerations of the Etiology of Compulsive Drug Use," *Journal of the American Psychoanalytic Association* 22 (1974): 820–843.

4. H. Krystal and H. A. Raskin, *Drug Dependence: Aspects of Ego Functions* (Detroit, Mich.: Wayne State University Press, 1970).

5. H. Wieder and E. Kaplan, "Drug Use in Adolescents," *Psychoanalytic Study of the Child* 24 (1969): 399–431.

6. H. Milkman and W. A. Frosch, "On the Preferential Abuse of Heroin and Amphetamine," *Journal of Nervous and Mental Disease* 156 (1973): 242–248.

7. E. J. Khantzian, "Self Selection and Progression in Drug Dependence," *Psychiatry Digest* 10 (1975): 19–22.

8. J. V. Spotts and F. C. Shontz, "Drug Induced Ego States: A Trajectory Theory of Drug Experience," *Society of Pharmacology* 1 (1987): 19–51.

9. N. Zinberg, *Drug, Set and Setting: The Basis for Controlled Intoxicant Use* (New Haven, Conn.: Yale University Press, 1984).

10. Zinberg, *Drug, Set and Setting.*

11. O. Fenichel, *The Psychoanalytic Theory of Neurosis* (New York: W. W. Norton, 1945).

12. Khantzian, "Self-Medication Hypothesis of Addictive Disorders"; Wurmser, "Psychoanalytic Considerations of the Etiology of Compulsive Drug Use"; Wieder and Kaplan, "Drug Use in Adolescents."

CHAPTER 7: SELF-MEDICATION, PSYCHIATRIC DISORDERS, AND EMOTIONAL PAIN

1. R. Glass, "Blue Mood, Blackened Lungs: Depression and Smoking," *Journal of the American Medical Association* 264 (1990): 1583–1584.

2. G. E. Vaillant and E. S. Milofsky, "The Etiology of Alcoholism: A Prospective Viewpoint," *American Psychologist* 37 (1982): 494–503. M. A. Schuckit and T. L. Smith, "An 8-year Follow-up of 450 Sons of Alcoholic and Control Subjects," *Archives of General Psychiatry* 53 (1996): 202–210.

3. M. H. Keeler, C. I. Taylor, and W. C. Miller, "Are All Recently Detoxified Alcoholics Depressed?" *American Journal of Psychiatry* 136 (1979): 586–588.

4. *Diagnostic and Statistical Manual of Mental Disorders*, 4th ed. (Washington, D.C.: American Psychiatric Association, 1994).

5. B. J. Rounsaville, M. M. Weissman, K. Crits-Cristoph, C. Wilber, and H. Kleber, "Diagnosis and Symptoms of Depression in Opiate Addicts: Course and Relationship to Treatment Outcome," *Archives of General Psychiatry* 39 (1982): 151–156; G. E. Woody, L. Luborsky, A. T. McLellan, C. P. O'Brien, A. T. Beck,

J. Blaine, et al. "Psychotherapy for Opiate Addicts: Does It Help?" *Archives of General Psychiatry* 40 (1983): 639–645; E. J. Khantzian and C. Treece, "DSM-III Psychiatric Diagnosis of Narcotic Addicts: Recent Findings," *Archives of General Psychiatry* 42 (1985): 1067–1071.

6. D. A. Regier, M. E. Farmer, D. S. Rae, B. Z. Locke, S. J. Keith, L. L. Judd, et al., "Comorbidity of Mental Disorders with Alcohol and Other Drug Abuse: Results from the Epidemiologic Catchment Area (ECA) Study," *Journal of the American Medical Association* 264 (1990): 2511–2518; R. C. Kessler, R. M. Crum, L. A. Warner, C. B. Nelson, et al., "Lifetime Co-occurrence of DSM-III-R Alcohol Abuse and Dependence with Other Psychiatric Disorders in the National Comorbidity Survey," *Archives of General Psychiatry* 54 (1997): 313–321.

7. R. C. Kessler, K. A. McGonagle, S. Zhao, et al., "Lifetime and 12-month Prevalence of DSM-III-R Psychiatric Disorders in the United States: Results from the National Comorbidity Survey," *Archives of General Psychiatry* 51 (1994): 8–19.

8. M. J. Albanese, W. Blair, D. DiRocco, et al., "Depression as a Predictor of Compliance with Substance Abuse Treatment" (poster presented at the Fifth Annual Research Day, Consolidated Department of Psychiatry, Harvard Medical School, Boston, Mass., March 12, 1997).

9. PDM Task Force, *Psychodynamic Diagnostic Manual* (Silver Spring, Md.: Alliance of Psychoanalytic Organizations, 2006).

10. B. J. Rounsaville, S. F. Anton, K. Carroll, et al., "Psychiatric Diagnoses of Treatment-Seeking Cocaine Abusers," *Archives of General Psychiatry* 48, no. 1 (1991): 43–51.

11. Kessler, McGonagle, Zhao, et al., "Lifetime and 12-month Prevalence of DSM-III-R Psychiatric Disorders in the United States."

12. H. J. Shaffer and G. B. Eber, "Temporal Progression of Cocaine Dependence Symptoms in the U.S. National Comorbidity Survey," *Addiction* 97, no. 5 (2002): 543–554.

13. Office of Applied Studies, *Results from the 2005 National Survey on Drug Use and Health: National Findings*, DHHS publication no. SMA 06-4194, NSDUH Series H-30 (Rockville, Md.: Substance Abuse and Mental Health Services Administration, 2006).

14. K. Graham, A. Massak, A. Demers, and J. Rehm, "Does the Association between Alcohol Consumption and Depression Depend on How They Are Measured?" *Alcoholism: Clinical and Experimental Research* 31, no. 1 (2007): 78.

15. D. M. Fergusson and L. J. Woodward, "Mental Health, Educational, and Social Role Outcomes of Adolescents with Depression," *Archives of General Psychiatry* 59, no. 3 (2002): 225–231.

16. M. J. Albanese and R. Pies, "The Bipolar Patient with Comorbid Substance Use Disorder," *CNS Drugs* 18, no. 9 (2004): 585–596.

17. R. D. Weiss, M. Kolodziej, M. L. Griffin, L. M. Najavits, et al., "Substance Use and Perceived Symptom Improvement among Patients with Bipolar

Disorder and Substance Dependence," *Journal of Affective Disorders* 79 (2004): 279–283.

18. S. C. Sonne, K. T. Brady, and W. A. Morton, "Substance Abuse and Bipolar Affective Disorder," *Journal of Nervous and Mental Disease* 182 (1994): 349–352.

19. R. D. Weiss, S. M. Mirin, J. L. Michael, and A. C. Sollogub, "Psychopathology in Chronic Cocaine Abusers," *American Journal of Drug and Alcohol Abuse* 12 (1986): 17–29; R. D. Weiss, S. M. Mirin, M. L. Griffin, and J. L. Michael, "Psychopathology in Cocaine Abusers: Changing Trends," *Journal of Nervous and Mental Disease* 176 (1988): 719–725.

20. K. P. Conway, W. Compton, F. S. Stinson, and B. F. Grant, "Lifetime Comorbidity of DSM-IV Mood and Anxiety Disorders and Specific Drug Use Disorders: Results from the National Epidemiologic Survey on Alcohol and Related Conditions," *Journal of Clinical Psychiarty* 67 (2006): 247–257.

21. S. E. Thomas, C. L. Randall, and M. H. Carrigan, "Drinking to Cope in Socially Anxious Individuals: A Controlled Study," *Alcoholism: Clinical and Experimental Research* 27, no. 12 (December 2003): 1937–1943.

22. J. Bolton, B. Cox, I. Clara, and J. Sareen, "Use of Alcohol and Drugs to Self-Medicate Anxiety Disorders in a Nationally Representative Sample," *Journal of Nervous and Mental Disease* 194, no. 11 (November 2006): 818–825.

23. K. P. Conway, W. Compton, F. S. Stinson, and B.F. Grant, "Lifetime Comorbidity of DSM-IV Mood and Anxiety Disorders and Specific Drug Use Disorders," *Journal of Clinical Psychiatry* 67 (2006): 247–257.

24. E. J. Khantzian, *Treating Addiction as a Human Process* (Northvale, N.J.: Jason Aronson, 1999), 262.

25. M. J. Albanese, E. J. Khantzian, S. I. Murphy, and A. I. Green, "Decreased Substance Use in Chronically Psychotic Patients Treated with Clozapine," *American Journal of Psychiatry* 151 (1994): 780–781.

26. J. van Os, M. Bak, M. Hanssen, et al., "Marijuana Use and Psychosis: A Longitudinal Population-based Study," *American Journal of Epidemiology* 156 (2002): 319–327.

27. M. F. Brunette, K. T. Mueser, H. Xie, and R. E. Drake, "Relationships between Symptoms of Schizophrenia and Substance Abuse," *Journal of Nervous and Mental Disease* 186, no. 1 (1997): 13–20.

28. L. Dixon, G. Haas, P. J. Weiden, et al., "Drug Abuse in Schizophrenic Patients: Clinical Correlates and Reasons for Use," *American Journal of Psychiatry* 148, no. 2 (1991): 224–230.

29. T. Wilens, S. V. Faraone, and J. Biederman, "Attention-Deficit/ Hyperactivity Disorder in Adults," *Journal of the American Medical Association* 292 (2004): 619–623.

30. Personal communication. His book *Driven to Distraction* (with John J. Ratey, Pantheon, New York, 1994) was important in drawing attention to ADHD in adults and its multiple manifestations and complications, including substance use disorders.

31. T. Wilens et al., "Does Stimulant Therapy of ADHD Beget Later Substance Abuse: A Metanalytic Review of the Literature," *Pediatrics* 11 (2003): 179–185.

32. E. J. Khantzian, "An Extreme Case of Cocaine Dependence and Marked Improvement with Methylphenidate Treatment," *American Journal of Psychiatry* 140 (1983): 784–785; E. J. Khantzian, F. Gawin, H. D. Kleber, et al., "Methylphenidate (Ritalin) Treatment of Cocaine Dependence: A Preliminary Report," *Journal of Substance Abuse Treatment* 1 (1984): 107–112.

33. Khantzian, "An Extreme Case of Cocaine Dependence," 784–785; Khantzian, Gawin, Kleber, et al., "Methylphenite (Ritalin) treatment," 107–112.

34. T. E. Wilens, M. C. Monuteaux, L. E. Snyder, et al., "The Clinical Dilemma of Using Medications in Substance-Abusing Adolescents and Adults with Attention-Deficit/Hyperactivity Disorder: What Does the Literature Tell Us?" *Journal of Child and Adolescent Psychopharmacology* 15, no. 5 (2005): 787–798; J. Mariana and F. Levin, "Workshop: Stimulant Pharmacotherapy in Patients with Substance Use Disorders" (American Academy of Addiction Psychiatry Annual Scientific Conference, St. Petersburg, Fla., December 2006).

CHAPTER 8: TRAUMA AND THE SELF-MEDICATION HYPOTHESIS

1. P. Ouimette and P. J. Brown, eds., *Trauma and Substance Abuse: Causes, and Consequences, and Treatment of Comorbid Disorders* (Washington, D.C.: American Psychological Association, 2002).

2. D. C. Ompad, R. M. Ikeda, N. Shah, C. M. Fuller, et al., "Childhood Sexual Abuse and Age at Initiation of Injection Drug Use," *American Journal of Public Health* 95 (2005): 703–709; H. W. Clark, C. L. Masson, K. L. Delucchi, et al., "Violent Traumatic Events and Drug Abuse Severity," *Journal of Substance Abuse Treatment* 20 (2001): 121–127; D. A. Hien, E. Nunes, F. R. Levin, and D. Fraser, "Posttraumatic Stress Disorder and Short-term Outcome in Early Methadone Treatment," *Journal of Substance Abuse Treatment* 19 (2000): 31–37.

3. R. E. Adams and J. A. Boscarino, et al., "Social and Psychological Resources and Health Outcomes after the World Trade Center Disaster," *Social Science and Medicine* 62, no. 1 (2006): 176–188.

4. J. L. Herman, *Trauma and Recovery: The Aftermath of Violence—from Domestic Abuse to Political Terror* (New York: Basic Books, 1997).

5. M. D. DeBellis, "Developmental Traumatology: A Contributory Mechanism for Alcohol and Substance Use Disorders," *Psychoneuroendocrinology* 27 (2002): 155–170.

6. H. Krystal, personal communication.

7. This case is a modified version of one previously reported in E. J. Khantzian, *Treating Addiction as a Human Process* (Northvale, N.J.: Jason Aronson, 1999).

8. N. Nehls and J. Sallmann, "Women Living with a History of Physical and/or Sexual Abuse, Substance Use, and Mental Health Problems," *Qualitative Health Research* 15, no. 3 (2005): 365–381.

CHAPTER 9: ADDICTION AND THE
PERPETUATION OF SUFFERING

1. K. Meninger, *Man against Himself* (New York: Free Press, 1935).
2. F. Schiffer, "Psychotherapy of Nine Successfully Treated Cocaine Abusers: Techniques and Dynamics," *Journal of Substance Abuse Treatment* 5 (1988): 131–137.
3. E. J. Khantzian, "Addiction: Self-destruction or Self-repair?" *Journal of Substance Abuse Treatment* 6 (1989): 75.
4. S. Rado, "The Psychoanalysis of Pharmacothymia," *Psychoanalytic Quarterly* 2 (1933): 1–23.
5. G. Sashin, personal communication.
6. H. Krystal, *Integration and Self-healing: Affect, Trauma, Alexithymia* (Hillsdale, N.J.: Analytic Press, 1988).
7. J. McDougall, "The 'Dis-affected' Patient; Reflections on Affect Pathology," *Psychoanalytic Quarterly* 1984: 386–409.
8. L. Wurmser, "Psychoanalytic Considerations of the Etiology of Compulsive Drug Use," *Journal of the American Psychoanalytic Association* 22 (1974): 820–843.
9. J. E. Gedo, *Conflict in Psychoanalysis: Essays in History and Method* (New York: Guilford Press, 1986).
10. S. Freud, "Beyond the Pleasure Principle," in *Standard Edition*, vol. 18 (London: Hogarth Press, 1955), 7–61.
11. W. R. Fairbairn, "Endopsychic Structures Considered in Terms of Object Relations," in *Psychoanalytic Studies of Personality* (London: Tavistock, 1952).
12. A. H. Modell, *Psychoanalysis in a New Context* (New York: International Universities Press, 1984), 34.
13. E. J. Khantzian and A. Wilson, "Substance Abuse, Repetition and the Nature of Addictive Suffering," in *Hierarchical Conceptions in Psychoanalysis*, ed. A. Wilson and J. E. Gedo, 263–283 (New York: Guilford Press, 1993).

CHAPTER 10: NICOTINE, MARIJUANA, AND THE SMH

1. S. Aldington et al., "The Effects of Marijuana on Pulmonary Structure, Function and Symptoms," *Thorax*, July 31, 2007, www.thorax.bmj.com/cgi/content/full/62/12/1058; J. M. Rey, "Does Marijuana Contribute to Psychotic Illness?" *Current Psychiatry* 6, no. 2 (2007): 36–47; L. Messinis, A. Kyprianidou, S.

Malefaki, and P. Papathanasopoulos, "Neuropsychological Deficits in Long-term Frequent Marijuana Users," *Neurology* 66 (2006): 737–739; P. Berghuis et al., "Hardwiring the Brain: Endocannabinoids Shape Neuronal Connectivity," *Science* 316, no. 5828 (2007): 1212–1216, www.sciencemag.org/cgi/content/abstract/316/5828/1212.

2. With the permission of Dr. Hughes, information presented at Gambling and Addiction Conference: Finding Common Ground on Prevention, Treatment, and Policy, Las Vegas, Nevada, December 7, 2005. The interested reader is referred to an excellent article by Dr. Hughes in which he elaborates on why nicotine is so addictive, especially in teens. His perspective is entirely consistent with the self-medication motives we emphasize in this book. J. R. Hughes, "Why Does Smoking so Often Produce Dependence? A Somewhat Different View," *Tobacco Control* 10 (2001): 62–64.

3. J. M. Schmitz and K. A. DeLaune, "Nicotine," in *Substance Abuse: A Comprehensive Textbook*, ed. J. H. Lowinson (Philadelphia: Lippincott Williams & Wilkins, 2005).

4. D. M. Ziedonis, T. R. Kosten, W. M. Glazer, and R. J. Frances, "Nicotine Dependence and Schizophrenia," *Hospital and Community Psychiatry* 54 (1994): 204–206.

5. D. M. Fergusson and L. J. Woodward, "Mental Health, Educational, and Social Role Outcomes of Adolescents with Depression," *Archives of General Psychiatry* 59, no. 3 (2002): 225–231.

6. R. F. Anda, D. F. Williamson, L. G. Escobedo, E. E. Mast, G. A. Giovino, and P. L. Remington, "Depression and the Dynamics of Smoking: A National Perspective," *Journal of the American Medical Association* 264 (1990): 1541–1545.

7. A. H. Glassman, J. E. Helzer, L. S. Covey, L. B. Cottler, F. Steiner, J. S. Tipp, et al., "Smoking, Smoking Cessation, and Major Depression," *Journal of the American Medical Association* 264 (1990): 1546–1549.

8. R. Glass, "Blue Mood, Blackened Lungs: Depression and Smoking," *Journal of the American Medical Association* 264 (1990): 1583–1584.

9. J. S. Brook, N. Yuming, and D. W. Brook, "Personality Risk Factors Associated with Trajectories of Tobacco Use," *American Journal of Addictions* 15 (2006): 426–433.

10. N. Breslau, M. M. Kilbey, and P. Andreski, "Vulnerability to Psychopathology in Nicotine Dependent Smokers: An Epidemiologic Study of Young Adults," *American Journal of Psychiatry* 150 (1993): 941–946.

11. L. Grinspoon and J. B. Bakalar, "Marihuana," in *Substance Abuse: A Comprehensive Textbook*, 3rd edition, ed. J. H. Lowinson, P. Ruiz, R. B. Millman, J. G. Langrod, 199–206 (Baltimore, Md.: Williams & Wilkins, 1997).

12. J. P. Chhatwal and K. J. Ressler, "Modulation of Fear and Anxiety by the Endogenous Cannabinoid System," *CNS Spectrums* 12, no. 3 (2007): 211–220.

13. A. G. Hohmann, R. L. Suplita, N. M. Bolton, M. Nathan, et al., "An Endocannabinoid Mechanism for Stress-induced Analgesia," *Nature* 435, no. 7045 (2005): 1108–1112.

14. M. T. Lynskey, A. L. Glowinski, A. A. Todorov, K. K. Bucholz, et al., "Major Depressive Disorder, Suicidal Ideation, and Suicide Attempt in Twins Discordant for Marijuana Dependence and Early-onset Marijuana Use," *Archives of General Psychiatry* 61 (2004): 1026–1032.

CHAPTER 11: BEHAVIORAL ADDICTIONS: DOES THE SMH APPLY?

1. Personal communication.
2. C. F. Gerwe, *The Orchestration of Joy and Suffering: Understanding Chronic Addiction* (New York; Algora Publishing, 2001).
3. J. H. Lowinson, P. Ruiz, R. B. Millman, and J. G. Langrod, *Substance Abuse: A Comprehensive Textbook* (New York: Lippincott Williams & Wilkins, 2005).
4. A. Goldberg, ed., *Errant Selves: A Casebook of Misbehavior* (Hillsdale, N.J.: Analytic Press, 2004).
5. A. Goldberg, ed., *Errant Selves: A Casebook of Misbehavior* (Hillsdale, N.J.: Analytic Press, 2004); S. Dowling, ed., *The Psychology and Treatment of Addictive Behavior* (New York: International University Press, 1995).
6. L. Dodes, *The Heart of Addiction* (New York: HarperCollins, 2002).
7. H. J. Shaffer, D. A. LaPlante, R. A. LaBrie, R. C. Kidman, and A. N. Donato, "Toward a Syndrome Model of Addiction: Multiple Expressions, Common Etiology," *Harvard Review of Psychiatry* 12 (2004): 367–374.
8. S. Rado, "The Psychoanalysis of Pharmacothymia," *Psychoanalysis Quarterly* 2 (1933): 1–23.

CHAPTER 12: THE NEUROBIOLOGY OF ADDICTION AND THE SMH

1. J. Panksepp, B. Knutson, and J. Burgdorf, "The Role of Brain Emotional Systems in Addictions: A Neuroevolutionary Perspective and New Self-Report Animal Model," *Addiction* 97 (2002): 459–469.
2. Y. L. Hurd, "Perspectives on Current Directions in the Neurobiology of Addiction Disorders Relevant to Genetic Risk Factors," *CNS Spectrum* 11, no. 11 (2006): 855–862.
3. R. Glass, "Blue Mood, Blackened Lungs: Depression and Smoking," *Journal of the American Psychological Association* 264, no. 12 (1990): 1583–1584.
4. G. F. Koob and M. LeMoal, "Drug Addiction, Dysregulation of Reward, and Allostasis," *Neuropsychopharmacology* 24 (2001): 97–129.
5. N. D. Volkow, J. S. Fowler, G. J. Wang, and J. M. Swanson, "Dopamine in Drug Abuse and Addiction: Results from Imaging Studies and Treatment Implications," *Molecular Psychiatry* no 9 (2004): 557–569.

6. G. Koob and M. J. Kreek, "Stress, Dysregulation of Drug Reward Pathways, and the Transition to Drug Dependence," *American Journal of Psychiatry* 164, no. 8 (2007): 1149–1159.

7. S. E. Hyman, "Addiction: A Disease of Learning and Memory," *American Journal of Psychiatry* 162 (2005): 1414–1422.

8. P. W. Kalivas, "Neurobiology of Cocaine Addiction: Implications for New Pharmacotherapy," *American Journal on Addictions* 16 (2007): 71–78.

9. S. C. Pandey, H. Zhang, A. Roy, and K. Misra, "Central and Medial Amygdaloid Brain-derived Neurotropic Factor Signaling Plays a Critical Role in Alcohol-drinking and Anxiety-like Behaviors," *Journal of Neuroscience* 26, no. 32 (2006): 8320–8331.

10. M. D. Lieberman, N. I. Eisenberger, M. J. Crockett, S. M. Tom, et al., "Putting Feelings into Words: Affect Labeling Disrupts Amygdala Activity in Response to Affective Stimuli," *Psychological Science* 18, no. 5 (2007): 421–427.

11. B. W. Dunlop and C. B. Nemeroff, "The Role of Dopamine in the Pathophysiology of Depression," *Archives of General Psychiatry* 64, no. 3 (2007): 327–337.

12. M. D. DeBellis, "Developmental Traumatology: A Contributory Mechanism for Alcohol and Substance Use Disorders," *Psychoneuroendocrinology* 27 (2002): 155–170.

13. T. R. Insel, "Is Social Attachment an Addictive Disorder?" *Physiology and Behavior* 79 (2003): 351–357.

14. A. Verdejo-Garcia, A. Bechara, E. C. Recknor, and M. Perez-Garcia, "Executive Dysfunction in Substance Dependent Individuals during Use and Abstinence: An Examination of the Behavioral, Cognitive and Emotional Correlates of Addiction," *Journal of the International Neuropsychological Society* 12 (2006): 405–415; A. Verdejo-Garcia, and M. Perez-Garcia "Ecological Assessment of Executive Functions in Substance Dependent Individuals," *Drug and Alcohol Dependence* 90, no. 1 (2007): 48–55.

15. B. J. Sadock, V. A. Sadock, "Psychological Factors Affecting Medical Conditions and Psychosomatic Medicine," in *Kaplan and Sadock's Synopsis of Psychiatry: Behavioral Science/Clinical Psychiatry*, 9th edition, ed. B. J. Sadock and V. A. Sadock (Philadelphia: Lippincott Williams & Wilkins, 2003).

CHAPTER 13: HOW THE SMH CAN GUIDE TREATMENT AND RECOVERY

1. Project MATCH Research Group, "Matching Alcoholism Treatments to Client Heterogeneity: Project MATCH Posttreatment Drinking Outcomes," *Journal of Studies on Alcohol* 58 (1997): 7–29.

2. E. P. Nace, "The Importance of Alcoholics Anonymous in Changing Destructive Behavior," *Primary Psychiatry* 10, no. 9 (2003): 65–68.

3. J. E. Mack, "Alcoholism, AA and the Governance of the Self," in *Dynamic Approaches to the Understanding and Treatment of Alcoholism*, ed. M. H. Bean and N. E. Zinberg, 128–162 (New York: Free Press, 1981); E. J. Khantzian and J. E. Mack, "AA and Contemporary Psychodynamic Theory," *Recent Developments in Alcoholism*, vol. 7, ed. M. Galanter, 67–89 (New York: Plenum, 1989); E. J. Khantzian and J. E. Mack, "How AA Works and Why It Is Important for Clinicians to Understand," *Journal of Substance Abuse Treatment* 11 (1994): 77–92.

4. G. E. Woody, A. T. McLellan, L. Luborsky, and C. P. O'Brien, "Psychotherapy for Substance Abuse," *Psychiatric Clinics of North America*, ed. S. M. Mirin, 9 (1986): 547–562.

5. E. J. Khantzian, K. S. Halliday, and W. E. McAuliffe, *Addiction and the Vulnerable Self: Modified Group Therapy for Substance Abusers* (New York: Guilford Press, 1990); E. J. Khantzian, *Treating Addiction as a Human Process* (Northvale, N.J.: Jason Aronson, 1999).

6. K. M. Carroll and L. S. Onken, "Behavioral Therapies for Drug Abuse," *American Journal of Psychiatry* 162 (2005): 1452–1460.

7. J. O. Prochaska and C. C. DiClemente, "Stages of Change in the Modification of Problem Behaviors," *Progress of Behavior Modification* 28 (1992): 183–218.

8. W. R. Miller and S. Rollnick, eds., *Motivational Interviewing: Preparing People for Change*, 2nd ed. (New York: Guilford Press, 2002).

9. E. J. Khantzian, S. J. Golden, and W. E. McAuliffe, "Group Therapy," in *Textbook of Substance Abuse Treatment*, 3rd ed., ed. M. Galanter and H. D. Kleber, 391–403 (Washington, D.C.: American Psychiatric Press, 2004). Khantzian, Halliday, and McAuliffe, *Addiction and the Vulnerable Self*.

10. E. J. Khantzian, "Reflections on Group Treatments as Corrective Experiences for Addictive Vulnerability," *International Journal of Group Psychotherapy* 51 (2001): 11–20.

11. A. T. McLellan, I. O. Arndt, D. S. Metzger, G. E. Woody, and C. P. O'Brien, "The Effects of Psychosocial Services in Substance Abuse Treatment," *Journal of the American Medical Association* 269 (1993): 1953–1959.

12. R. D. Weiss, M. L. Griffin, S. F. Greenfield, et al., "Group Therapy for Patients with Bipolar Disorder and Substance Dependence: Results of a Pilot Study," *Journal of Clinical Psychiatry* 61 (2000): 361–367.

13. J. F. Kauffman, "Methadone Treatment and Recovery for Opioid Dependence," *Primary Psychiatry* 10, no. 9 (2003): 61–64.

14. M. J. Albanese and H. J. Shaffer, "Treatment Considerations in Patients with Addictions," *Primary Psychiatry* 10, no. 9 (2003): 55–60.

15. B. A. Johnson, N. Ait-Daoud, C. L. Bowden, C. C. DiClemente, et al., "Oral Topiramate for Treatment of Alcohol Dependence: A Randomized Controlled Trial," *Lancet* 361 (2003): 1677–1685.

16. M. J. Albanese and H. J. Shaffer, "Treatment Considerations in Patients with Addictions," *Primary Psychiatry* 10, no. 9 (2003): 55–60.

CHAPTER 14: CONCLUSION

1. E. J. Khantzian, "A Clinical Perspective of the Cause-Consequence Controversy in Alcoholic and Addictive Suffering," *Journal of the American Academy of Psychoanalysis* 15, no. 4 (1987): 521–537.

2. R. J. Frances, "The Wrath of Grapes versus the Self-Medication Hypothesis," *Harvard Review of Psychiatry* 4, no. 5 (1997): 287–289; R. Glass, "Blue Mood, Blackened Lungs: Depression and Smoking," *Journal of the American Medical Association* 264, no. 12 (1990): 1583–1584.

Selected References

Albanese, Mark J., and Howard J. Shaffer. "Treatment Considerations in Patients With Addictions." *Primary Psychiatry* no. 10 (Sept. 2003): 55–60.

Carroll, Kathleen M., and Lisa S. Onken. "Behavioral Therapies for Drug Abuse." *American Journal of Psychiatry* 162 no. 8 (August 2005): 1452–60.

Dodes, Lance. *The Heart of Addiction*. New York: HarperCollins, 2002.

Dowling, Scott, ed. *The Psychology and Treatment of Addictive Behavior*. New York: International University Press, 1995.

Erickson, Carlton K. *The Science of Addiction: From Neurobiology to Treatment*. New York: W.W. Norton, 2007.

Flores, Philip J. *Addiction as an Attachment Disorder*. Lanham, MD: Jason Aronson, 2004.

Frances, Richard J., Sheldon I. Miller, and Avram H. Mack, eds. *Clinical Textbook of Addictive Disorders*, 3rd ed. New York: Guilford Press, 2005.

Galanter, Marc, and Herbert Kleber, eds. *Textbook of Substance Use Treatment*, 4th ed. Washington, DC: American Psychiatric Press Inc., 2008.

Goldberg, Arnold, ed. *Errant Selves: A Casebook of Misbehavior*. Hillsdale, NJ: The Analytic Press, 2000.

Herman, Judith L. *Trauma and Recovery: The Aftermath of Violence—From Domestic Abuse to Political Terror*. New York: Basic Books, 1997.

Hyman, Steven E. "Addiction: A Disease of Learning and Memory." *American Journal of Psychiatry* 162, no. 8 (August 2005):1414–22.

Kauffman, Janice F. "Methadone Treatment and Recovery for Opioid Dependence." *Primary Psychiatry* 10 no. 9 (Sept. 2003):61–64.

Khantzian, Edward J. *Treating Addiction as a Human Process*. Northvale, NJ: Jason Aronson, 1999.

Khantzian, Edward J., Kurt S. Halliday, and William E. McAuliffe. *Addiction and the Vulnerable Self: Modified Dynamic Group Therapy for Substance Abusers*. New York and London: Guilford Press, 1990.

149

Koob, George, and Mary J. Kreek. "Stress, Dysregulation of Drug Reward Pathways, and the Transition to Drug Dependence." *American Journal of Psychiatry* 164 no. 8 (August 2007):1149–59.

Lowinson, Joyce H., Pedro P. Ruiz, Robert B. Millman, and John G. Langrod, eds. (2005). *Substance Abuse: A Comprehensive Textbook.* Philadelphia: Lippincott Williams & Williams, 4th ed., 2005.

McLellan, A.Thomas, Isabelle O. Arndt, David S. Metzger, George E.Woody, and Charles P. O'Brien. "The Effects of Psychosocial Services in Substance Abuse Treatment." *Journal of the American Medical Association* 269 no. 4 (April 1993):1953–59.

Miller, William R., and Stephen Rollnick, eds. *Motivational Interviewing: Preparing People for Change.* 2nd ed. New York: Guilford Press, 2002.

Nace, Edward P., and Joyce A. Tinsley. *Patients with Substance Abuse Problems: Effective Identification, Diagnosis, and Treatment.* New York: W.W. Norton, 2007.

Ouimette, Paige, and Pamela J. Brown, eds. *Trauma and Substance Abuse: Causes, and Consequences, and Treatment of Comorbid Disorders.* Washington, DC: American Psychological Association, 2003.

Petry, N. M. *Pathological Gambling: Etiology, Comorbidity, and Treatment.* Washington, DC: American Psychological Association, 2005.

Prochaska, James O., and Carlo C. DiClemente. "Stages of Change in the Modification of Problem Behaviors." *Progress in Behavior Modification.* 28(1992): 183–218

Shaffer, Howard J., Debi A. LaPlante, Richard A. LaBrie, Rachel C. Kidman, Anthony N. Donato, and Michael V. Stanton. "Toward a Syndrome Model of Addiction: Multiple Expressions, Common Etiology." *Harvard Review of Psychiatry* 12 no. 6 (Nov./Dec.2004):367–74.

Vaillant, George E., and E. S. Milofsky. "The Etiology of Alcoholism: A Prospective Viewpoint." *American Psychologist* 37 (1982):494–503.

Walant, Karen B. *Creating the Capacity for Attachment: Treating Addictions and the Alienated Self.* Northvale, NJ: Jason Aronson Inc., 1995.

Weegman, Martin, and Robert Cohen., eds. *The Psychodynamics of Addiction.* London: Whurr Publishers, 2002.

Weiss, Roger D., Margaret L. Griffin, Shelly F. Greenfield, et al. "Group Therapy for Patients with Bipolar Disorder and Substance Dependence: Results of a Pilot Study." *Journal of Clinical Psychiatry* 61 (2000):361–67.

Wilens, Timothy, Stephen V. Faraone, and Joseph Biederman. "Attention-Deficit/Hyperactivity Disorder in Adults." *Journal of the American Medical Association* 292 no. 8 (August 2004):619–23.

Zinberg, Norman. *Drug, Set, and Setting: The Basis for Controlled Intoxicant Use.* New Haven, CT: Yale University Press, 1984.

Index

About the Authors

Edward J. Khantzian, a founding member of the department of psychiatry at Cambridge Health Alliance, is Clinical Professor of Psychiatry, Harvard Medical School, and Associate Chief of Psychiatry at Tewksbury Hospital. He is President and Chairman of the Board of Directors of Physician Health Services, a subsidiary of the Massachusetts Medical Society. He received his BA in psychology from Boston University and his MD from Albany Medical College, completed training in psychiatry at Massachusetts Mental Center, and is a graduate of the Boston Psychoanalytic Society and Institute. Dr. Khantzian is one of the founders of the American Academy of Addiction Psychiatry and is a past-president of that organization.

Mark J. Albanese is Director of Addictions Treatment Services at Cambridge Health Alliance, and Assistant Clinical Professor of Psychiatry at Harvard Medical School. He attended Harvard College and Cornell University Medical College. He did his internship in medicine at Brigham and Women's Hospital, and his psychiatry residency at Massachusetts Mental Health Center. He is certified by the American Board of Psychiatry and Neurology in general psychiatry and addiction psychiatry.